THE TOUCH OF TIME

Stewart Conn was born in Glasgow and grew up in Ayrshire, with his adulthood split between Glasgow and Edinburgh where he now lives. These locations, and the Scottish Islands, provide a vivid social and familial backdrop for much of his poetry; while several sequences set in France and Italy respond to works of art.

His early collections *Stoats in the Sunlight* (1968), *An Ear to the Ground* (1972) and *Under the Ice* (1978) were published by Hutchinson, the first also appearing as *Ambush & Other Poems* (Macmillan, New York, 1970). His later collections have all been published by Bloodaxe Books: *In the Kibble Palace* (1987), *The Luncheon of the Boating Party* (1992) and *In the Blood* (1995); followed by a selected volume *Stolen Light* (1999), *Ghosts at Cockcrow* (2005), *The Breakfast Room* (2010), and *The Touch of Time: New & Selected Poems* (2014).

Other publications include *Distances* (Scottish Cultural Press, 2001) and, as editor, *100 Favourite Scottish Poems* (Scottish Poetry Library/Luath Press, 2006) and *100 Favourite Scottish Love Poems* (Luath Press, 2008). Among his published plays are *I Didn't Always Live Here, The King, The Burning, The Aquarium, Thistlewood, Play Donkey, Herman* and *Hugh Miller*.

He has received awards from the Eric Gregory Trust, the Scottish Arts Council and the Society of Authors, an English-Speaking Union Thynne travel scholarship and the Institute of Contemporary Scotland's inaugural Iain Crichton Smith award. *An Ear to the Ground* was a Poetry Book Society Choice, *Stolen Light* was shortlisted for Saltire Book of the Year and *The Breakfast Room* was the 2011 Scottish Poetry Book of the Year.

Stewart Conn's website: www.stewartconn.com

STEWART CONN

The Touch of Time

NEW & SELECTED POEMS

BLOODAXE BOOKS

Copyright © Stewart Conn 1967, 1968, 1972, 1978, 1987,
1992, 1995, 1999, 2001, 2005, 2007, 2010, 2012, 2014

ISBN: 978 1 85224 998 4

First published 2014 by
Bloodaxe Books Ltd,
Highgreen,
Tarset,
Northumberland NE48 1RP.

www.bloodaxebooks.com
For further information about Bloodaxe titles
please visit our website or write to
the above address for a catalogue

Supported by
ARTS COUNCIL
ENGLAND

Cover design: Neil Astley & Pamela Robertson-Pearce.

Printed in Great Britain by Bell & Bain Limited, Glasgow, Scotland,
on acid-free paper sourced from mills with FSC chain of custody certification.

for Judy

Dame, de qui toute ma joie vient…
GUILLAUME DE MACHAUT, *c.* 1300-77

ACKNOWLEDGEMENTS

Sections I-VII are extracted from *Stolen Light: Selected Poems* (Bloodaxe Books, 1999), which in turn drew on *Thunder in the Air* (Akros, Preston, 1967) and *The Chinese Tower* (MacDonald, Edinburgh, 1967); *Stoats in the Sunlight* (1968), *An Ear to the Ground* (1972) and *Under the Ice* (1978), all Hutchinson, London; *In the Kibble Palace* (Bloodaxe Books, 1987), *At the Aviary* (Snail Press, Plumstead, South Africa, 1992), and *The Luncheon of the Boating Party* (1992) and *In the Blood* (1995), both Bloodaxe Books. Other poems are reinstated from these volumes or are from *Distances: a personal evocation of people and places* (Scottish Cultural Press, 2001). The poems tend to be grouped thematically rather than observing strict chronology. A number of revisions and excisions have been made.

Sections VIII and IX represent respectively *Ghosts at Cockcrow* (2005) and *The Breakfast Room* (2010), both from Bloodaxe and the latter incorporating *The Loving-Cup* (Mariscat Press, 2007). Section X includes poems from *Estuary* (Mariscat Press, 2012).

Gratitude is expressed to all the publishers named and, for poems in the final Section or hitherto unacknowledged, to the editors of *Carapace, Edinburgh Review, The Herald, New Writing Scotland, The North, Poetry International* (San Diego), *Poetry Scotland, The Scotsman, The Scottish Review of Books, Southlight, The Spectator* and *The Times Literary Supplement*.

Special thanks to Hamish Whyte for discerning guidance.

CONTENTS

I

Todd

My father's white uncle became
   arthritic and testamental in
   lyrical stages. He held cardinal sin
was misuse of horses, then any game

won on the sabbath. A Clydesdale
   to him was not bells and sugar or declension
   from paddock, but primal extension
of rock and soil. Thundered nail

turned to sacred bolt. And each night
   in the stable he would slaver and slave
   at cracked hooves, or else save
bowls of porridge for just the right

beast. I remember I lied
   to him once, about oats: then I felt
   the brand of his loving tongue, the belt
of his own horsey breath. But he died,

when the mechanised tractor came to pass.
   Now I think of him neighing to some saint
   in a simple heaven or, beyond complaint,
leaning across a fence and munching grass.

Ferret

More vicious than stoat or weasel
because caged, kept hungry, the ferrets
were let out only for the kill:
an alternative to sulphur and nets.

Once one, badly mauled, hid
behind a treacle-barrel in the shed.
Throwing me back, Matthew slid
the door shut. From outside

the window, I watched. He stood
holding an axe, with no gloves.
Then it sprang; and his sleeves
were drenched in blood

where the teeth had sunk. I hear
its high-pitched squeal,
the clamp of its neat steel
jaws. And I remember

how the axe flashed, severing
the ferret's head,
and how its body kept battering
the barrels, long after it was dead.

Farm

The sun drills the shire through and through
till the farm is a furnace, the yard
a quivering wickerwork of flame. Pitchforks
rise and fall, bales are fiery ingots.
Straws sputter like squibs. Stones
explode. From the byre, smack on time,
old Martha comes clattering out
with buttered bannocks and milk in a pail.

Todd, his face ablaze, swims back
in what shadow there is. Hugh and John
stretch out among sheaves. Hens squabble
for crusts; a dog flicks its tail
at a cleg; blueflies bunch like grapes.
Still the sun beats down, a hammer
on tin. And high overhead vapour-trails
drift seaward, out past Ailsa Craig.

Harelaw

Ploughlands roll where limekilns lay
   seeping in craters. Where once dense
   fibres oozed against gatepost and fence
till staples burst, firm wheatfields sway;
   and where quarries reeked, intense

with honeysuckle, a truck dumps load
   upon load of earth, of ash and slag
   for the raking. Spliced hawsers drag
roots out and wrench the rabbit wood
   apart as though some cuckoo fugue

had rioted. On this mossy slope
   that raindrops used to drill and drum
   through dusk, no nightjar flits nor numb
hawk hangs as listening foxes lope
   and prowl; no lilac shadows thumb

the heavy air. This holt was mine
   to siege and plunder, here I caged
   rare beasts or swayed royally on the aged
backs of horses – here hacked my secret sign,
   strode, wallowed, ferreted, rampaged.

But acres crumple and the farm's new image
   spreads over the old. As I face
   its change, a truck tips litter; hens assess
bright tins, then peck and squawk their rage.
   The truck spurts flame and I have no redress.

Country Dance

Before the advent of the combine
the big mill would lumber from farm
to farm, spouting steam and flame:
stooks extending to the horizon
and beyond, weathered by sun or rain.

Intricate as a dance, was the tying
of the sheaves, on the ground
or against one thigh, to a communal
rhythm; then their hoisting
in the stackyard, forks flashing;

and as though riding on air,
the man on top, under steady
bombardment, circling and weaving,
gold ramparts rising round him
to a music compelling as any eightsome.

Ayrshire Farm

Every new year's morning the farmers
would meet at Harelaw with their guns
for the shoot. Mungo red in the face,
Matthew hale as a tree, John huge
in old leather. The others in dribs
and drabs, shotguns over their shoulders,
bags flopping at their sides, collars up.

We'd set out across the north park,
the glaur on our leggings freezing
as we left the shelter of the knowes.
No dogs. Even the ferrets on this day
of days left squealing behind
their wire. We'd fan out, taking
the slope at a steady tramp.

Mungo always aimed first, blasting away
at nothing. Hugh cursed under his breath;
the rest of us kept going. Suddenly
the hares would rise from the bracken-clumps
and go looping uphill. I remember
the banks alive with scuts, the dead
gorse-tufts splattered with shot.

One by one the haversacks filled,
the blood dripping from them, staining
the snow. Matthew still in front,
directing the others; the sun red
behind its dyke, the wind rising.
And myself bringing up the rear,
pretending I was lost, become the quarry.

Three blasts on a whistle, the second
time round. And in from the sleet,
we would settle on bales with bottles
and flasks, to divide the spoils. The bodies
slit, and hung on hooks to drip. The rest
thrown smoking on the midden. The dogs
scrabbling at their chains, Todd's stallion

rearing at the reek of blood. Then in
to the fire and a roaring new year:
Old Martha and Mima scuffling to and fro,
our men's bellies filling, hands
slowly thawing. And for me, off to bed,
a pig in the sheets, the oil lamp
throwing shadows of rabbits on the wall.

*

Last winter I covered the same ground
on my own, no gun. Martha and Mima
have gone to rest. Todd has tethered
his horses under the hill. Mungo too,
from a fall at the baling. Yet my breathing
seemed to make their shapes; and Matthew's
and Hugh's, and my own bringing up the rear.

At the road-end I stopped and stood
for some time, just listening. My hands
growing numb. Then I crossed the track
to where a single rabbit lay twitching,
big-headed, eyes bulging, in pain.
I took the heaviest stone I could find;
and with one blow beat in its brains.

Todd

a sequence

I

I can still see him at the head of the byre:
the cloth cap, the clogs tipped with steel,
the stool under one arm, the red hands.

Or shuffling from stall to stall, religiously
humped. Feet splaying the pail, one cheek
against the belly of the beast. Later on

in the kitchen, over porridge and cream,
his talk all of Jacob, of Moses
and Aaron, of Daniel in the lions' den.

The front room hung with prints of horses,
paintings of himself in trap and gig.
On the sideboard, the silver cups he had won.

When his turn came he lay a long time ill,
his skull shining, the mind fumbling
to a conclusion of its own. Not complaining.

Could it really be he did not notice
his shadow diminishing against the wall,
his skin going the colour of wasted grain?

II

For three days and nights the stallion
lay shivering in its stall. Two nights
running, Todd stayed in the stable

mopping the fever up, packing blankets
and straw, trying a mixture of bran
and mash, all other tricks failing.

The beams stretched and shrank. The lamp
hissed. Next morning the byremen brought
ropes, and hauled. The dead weight slumped.

Nothing could get it to its feet. The breath
rotten, the flanks acid, its hindquarters
done. The vet came, in a yellow coat.

As he reached the door the stallion
came shuddering upright, head forking, eyes
huge and rolling, hooves flint on stone.

When it had been put down, Todd undid
his leggings, coughing up green rheum, asking why
each time the vet came a good beast had to die.

III

The yard is littered with scrap, with axles
and tyres, buckled hoops and springs – all rusting.
The wreckage of cars that have been dumped.

The hut is still there. In the doorway
two men talk horses – but not as he did
in the days when the Clydesdales came

to be shod, the milk-wagons for repair.
The din of iron on iron brings it all back:
Rob beating the anvil, to a blue flame;

the beast straining, the bit biting in,
horn burning, the sour tang of iron,
the sizzling, the perfect fit of the shoe.

In his mind's eye, the whole yard is teeming
with horses, ducking blackthorn, tails
swishing, the gates behind them clanging…

The men have started to strip an old van.
In passing he takes a kick at the wing. No one
notices. The dead metal does not ring at all.

IV

How he would stroke their muzzles, haul their brute
heads back, drive and pinion them against
the stable wall, throw round them bright chains.

Then bring armfuls of hay, water slopping
from buckets, oats stirred in a tub. Their breath
pounding round him, like bursts of steam.

One shoulder bent; his hands covered with sores,
with hacks and blisters, the marks of horses.
Still he combed them, pared hooves, dried the rank

sweat up. For whose sake he was lamed, gave up
meat and drink, lost sleep; with no thought
for the swifts in the eaves, the clegs pricking

the blood, the rats in the straw. I still see him
come cantering out to the yard, his brown serge
suit streaming, the horses under him neighing

and neighing. No more than half real. At once
fabulous and absurd. Like Goya, who went painting
at night with candles round the rim of his hat.

Reading Matter

The *Glasgow Herald*, delivered on week-days,
read avidly for its front-page obituaries
and financial news. Saturday's
Standard gave the cattle-mart prices.

Both would end up wrapping cheese pieces
carried out to the fields in wicker baskets
by great-aunts wearing frayed straw hats,
as gravely as though they bore the loaves and fishes.

All that was permitted on Sundays, the Bible.
But each month a splash of colour –
National Geographic, its yellow cover
garish against the patterned wallpaper

And the *People's Friend* once a week
to be pored over in private
then reappear torn into squares, stuck
on a metal hook in the outside toilet.

Stoats in the Sunlight

I once came across a pack of stoats in the sunlight,
    their eyes like jewels, the tips of their tails black.

One kept swinging on a fencepost and springing
    to the ground, leaving the wires twanging.

As at a word of command, they took up
    close formation and moved off in one direction.

Knowing what I do now, I wouldn't have stood there
    watching, imagining them such dainty playthings.

The Shed

When the milking was done, the byre
mucked out, and the cows bedded
for the night, I would creep to the shed
where the billy-goat was tethered

behind the bales. His hooves danced
as we fought, striking sparks
as I swung him by the scruff or had him
by the beard, butting and kicking.

Now and then a whinny, as he shook himself
free. His skull brick-hard, the eyes
twists of straw. Or I'd force cow-cake
on him: his stench filling the shed.

The farm has changed hands twice.
Last week I visited it, the first
time in years. As I passed the shed
a chain clanged – and I leapt aside

suddenly terrified that the goat
(or his wrinkled ghost) might come
slithering over the straw-bales,
pinning me back with his yellow eye.

Forebears

My father's uncle was the fastest
thing on two wheels, sitting in a gig,
the reins tight, his back at an angle
of thirty degrees, puffing up dust-clouds
as he careered down Craigie Hill.

His father before him, the strongest man
in Ayrshire, took a pair of cartwheels
by the axle and walked off with them: I have
visions of him in the meadow, holding
two ropes, a stallion straining on each.

Before that, no doubt, we boasted
the straightest furrow, the richest yield.
No measurements needed: each farm
bore its best, as each tree its fruit.
We even had a crazy creature in crinolines

who locked her letters in a brass box.
Others too ... but what do such truths
add up to – when the nearest
(and furthest) I get is visiting
their elaborately cared-for graves?

On an adjoining stone are a skull
and hourglass, from Covenanter
days. Their lives a duller
sacrifice. John on his moral staff,
the great-aunts with their rigid ways,

smacking of goodness in the strictest
sense, members of a sect, Elect almost,
shared surely something of flint
in the brain: their mortal goal
salvation, through purification of the soul.

On Craigie Hill

The farmhouse seems centuries ago,
the steadings slouched under a sifting of snow
for weeks on end, lamps hissing, logs stacked
like drums in the shed, the ice having to be cracked
to let the shaggy cats drink. Or
back from the mart through steaming pastures

men would come riding – their best
boots gleaming, rough tweeds pressed
to a knife-edge, pockets stuffed with notes.

Before that even, I could visualise (from coloured
prints) traps rattling, wheels spinning; furred
figures posing like sepia dolls
in a waxen world of weddings and funerals.
When Todd died, last of the old stagers,
friends of seventy years followed the hearse.
Soon the farm went out of the family: the Cochranes
going to earth or like their cousins
deciding it was time to hit town.

The last link broken, the farm-buildings stand
in a clutter below the quarry. The land
retains its richness – but in other hands.
Kilmarnock has encroached. It is hard to look
back with any sense of belonging.
Too much has changed, is still changing.
This blustery afternoon on Craigie Hill
I regard remotely the muddy track
my father used to trudge along, to school.

Craggy Country

Tales of Craigie Hill occupy my memory:
how at Mungo Farquhar's corner a pony
and trap, come recklessly adrift, sent driver
and passenger plummeting; the crazed beast,
flecked with foam, finally caught and quietened
outside the creamery, at Riccarton road-end.

I would think of this, as among empty churns
or clinging to the tailgate, I ascended
through morning mist to the farm: those
earlier generations like speeded-up figures
in Chaplin films, the frame frozen on Sundays,
men's boots gleaming, women in black lace.

Later on my second-hand Raleigh racer
with drop handle-bars I'd zigzag uphill,
squirming on the narrow saddle; on the return
journey imagining I was the first Scot
ever to win the Tour de France. Once,
eager to catch the cricket at Kirkstyle,

I cut things too fine and leaving my machine
described an arc in mid-air, in slow motion,
before landing; then headed painfully home
with the crumpled wheels and buckled frame
all grass and mud – object of derision
as townie come a cropper, or country buffoon.

Family Tree

In faded photographs, vanished generations
display shovel beards and gold watch-chains.
Here and there a sheepish smile, but in the main
they confront the future with old-fashioned
steadfastness of gaze. Flanked by cousins, austere
in their Sunday best, stands my great-uncle.

Churchill to him a warmonger, Stalin the Red Dragon
of the Apocalypse, he'd recite chapter and verse,
the Big Bible on his knee. On receiving the Gift
of Utterance from the Holy Ghost, he and his sisters
burst in on my father, studying for the ministry:
the World would end at noon next day: would he climb

Craigie Hill with them, to pray. They succeeded, unaided,
in keeping the Last Trump at bay. Thereafter
going into retreat – Martha 'staying with friends'
for a spell; the matter unlikely to have been
spoken of again, had not Todd on his death-bed
complained of '…live coals in the brain'.

Farm Funeral

His hearse should have been drawn by horses.
That's what he envisaged: the strain
and clop of crupper and chain, flashing
brass, fetlocks forcing high. With below
him, the frayed sheets turning slowly yellow.

On the sideboard a silver cup he had won,
inscribed 'to Todd Cochrane', now a lamp;
and tinted prints of his trotting days,
switch in hand, jockey-capped, the gig silky
with light, wheels exquisitely spinning.

For fifty years he was a breeder of horses;
nursing them nightly, mulling soft praise
long after the vet would have driven his plunger in.
Yet through them was his hip split. Twice
he was crushed by a stallion rearing.

Himself to the end unbroken. God's tool, yes,
that to earth will return. But not before time.
He ought to have been conveyed to the grave
by clattering Clydesdales, not cut off
from lark and sorrel by unseemly glass.

The shire is sprinkled with his ashes.
The fields are green through his kind. Their clay,
his marrow. As much as the roisterer, he: even
that last ride to Craigie, boots tightly laced,
his tie held in place by a diamond pin.

II

Afternoon

I lying on lichen can see
rivulets glancing in the sun
like fishes' scales or silver
sixpences. I rise and run

downhill until I reach a pool
wedged innocently between
two rocks, where lazy lizards slide
as if afraid of being seen

by heron or tell-tale poet. Then
a tasselled waterfall
that holds its breath only to spill
spindrift my thoughts. Suddenly all

grows quiet, as if today
as fossil has been overlapped
by some tomorrow only five
senses away but not yet mapped.

Thunder in the Air

On an evening fuzzy with heat
    and steeped in honey, I tear
through bracken: the threat
    of thunder hangs on stillest air.

Cows slump in pastures, crop
    pale clover, are yapped at
by threadbare dogs. Ponies droop
    across gateposts for the night.

The lark in upper reaches slips
    through song too pure to formalise,
unhinges dizzily, and flypes
    back to its dewy cage of grass.

Grey smirr of squirrel
    disappears up a pine tree –
stays in the abstract till
    showers of gold-dust give it away.

A breathless light bristles
    down branches, probes fur
from ferns. There is
    no need for disguises here,

and no need to reveal
    the beauty of this place.
I lift my head, and feel
    the huge rain slurping on my face.

Under Creag Mhor

A lizard fidgets in the sun
    that stuns it. Inchlong
    and perfect, agile among
pebbles, it purls its reflection

in crinkling pools. Neither
    freak nor fossil but something
    of each, legends clang
in its speck of a brain, roar

it down at no notice through brown
    peat juice, through mire
    of yellow bogland to where
it discovers its origin.

The bracken scurrs of Creag Mhor,
    pleated with clear water,
    no longer house dinosaur
and plated myth. But far

down, in the cool bright
   element of lizard's tiny
   being, in its ancient eye,
such monsters huddle yet.

In a Simple Light

Winter in this place
is a tangerine sun.
Against the skyline
nine Shetland ponies

stand like cut-outs
fraying at the edges.
Snow puffs and flurries
in weightless driblets

as they platter downhill,
pink-hooved, chins
stitched with frost, manes
jiggling a tinsel trail.

They clutter and jolt,
are pluff-bellied, biff
posts, thrum their trough
with warm breathing, smelt

ice. On the skyline
again, part fancy, they
freeze. In each eye
is a tangerine sun...

Setting

Strathglass, a confusion
    of colour. Broom and gorse
are transfiguration
    of yellow and gold. Furze

flames, myrtle steeps, is
    its singing fragrance. In
dusty silences, bees
    are pelted with pollen.

A breathless light
    thins and dribbles,
and haloes a mountain-goat
    maddened by midges. He nimbles

uphill, but falters as
    his shadow crops mine.
Poised, he sees
    me as shambling clown

invading his own.
    Then, gaelic mandarin,
he stilts over the sun.
    My gauze shadow is gone.

Margins

It is one thing to talk of terror
in the abstract, quite another
to face up to the particular,
fencing in a feeling of fear.

To speak say, of a mother
whose breast is touched by tumour;
or the less explicit horror
of a brother's mental disorder.

And most of all, in a rare
moment, to explain to a daughter
what margins are; the nature
of the charmed lives we bear.

The Chinese Tower

I

Hard land and dry, yet already
the lavender-clumps are bristling
like hassocks for Provençal ladies.

Crickets cross and uncross their legs.
The pine-slopes are musty. Soon
the valley will turn as on a spit.

In this world of bells, of goats
heavily thonged, thyme tracking
the tree-line, so single-minded

do the senses become that for them
the only escape is trussed brutally
to the bellies of great beasts.

II

But under rain, the land
is tin. There is brimstone
among the mountains.

Watertroughs overflow
like basins of wine.
Lightning fills the street.

Then two men with umbrellas
and between them
fifty sheep whose bells

are the din of a drowned
city. Now they are gone.
The crickets, too, are silent.

III

In as never before such blueness
(though to them the merest
translation of summer) two huntsmen

traverse the valley. They tack
as one, as yachts evenly paced;
though here in no breeze, but welter

of blueness. Even time can be treated
in terms of colour: nor arises
matter of identity. The cricket's

disguise, the butterfly fired
from slate – these are proof,
and part, of the same. You doubt it?

Watch then those huntsmen
scouring that hill. Watch them
halt, as one. Watch an arm

rise, and fall. And wait,
the length of the valley away,
for the sound of rushing stone.

IV

Or I find you, in a straw hat,
chasing butterflies. Even they
stress the oneness of it all

whose every movement is irretrievable
yet infinitely repeated. Such
is the truth not of this place only

but of things – hence of things
in this place. A bluetail shimmers
in a specific, no mere casual sun.

V

The waters of a mountain stream
assume the shape of ravine, then
create ravines of their own

in air. This in accordance
with the natural freedom
of things. And the village pump

always runs, a silver thread.
Ravine and rich chasm in one,
its surface is a source of light.

VI

High among pines, on a hill
overlooking the chapel, is a Chinese
tower. In both name, and style.

Behind it a viper lies coiled.
Is he lord of this place?
Has he an enquiring mind?

But the pines change from green
to smoky blue. Already there is
a chill in the air. Questions

need no answer. In absence
the presence of snake grows
strangely stronger. This square

of stone: an outlook tower.
Yet from few places can it be seen.
Certainly from nowhere in the village.

VII

Of the tower three things
are commonly said. That
at its base is a well

of pure water (this being
open to proof). That formerly
a tunnel led underground

to the village (this
to be taken on trust).
And thirdly that once,

in time of fire, monks
went dripping like candle-wax
down the face of the rock.

VIII

From the Chinese tower can be seen
the swerve of the valley, the lavender
fields and the mountains, pink

beyond. With finger in air
you can trace the tracks
of ravines, mark the pantiled roofs

of houses, of lofts, of the church
that strikes every hour twice.
And slowly, the blueness becomes

penetrable. There must always
be just such a place – its
tiny bells chinking in the wind.

[Thorame, Provence]

Old Actor

Not the same nowadays. They don't play
Shakespeare properly – not the way
we used to. Too superior
for a frontcloth, that's their

trouble. Opera use it, why not Theatre?
I mean, take the first scene from *Caesar* –
that ought to be played out front, the main
area set for the procession.

As for *Hamlet*, a gravedigger here
or there hardly matters any more.
(I saw Benson, as the Prince,
carried off after 'The rest is silence' –

but that *improved* the text.) Donat,
Martin-Harvey... what *style*. Another thing,
we'd always an orchestra in the pit
for the Bard – no loudspeaker in the wings.

Stage effects too: real waterfalls,
you name it – even Skegness,
still the gas floats. All they want these
days in a lad is, well you know ... *balls*.

Not that I'm against manliness,
anything of the sort. Bawdry for that matter.
I just think there are other
things that count, *besides* filling a codpiece.

North Uist

I

My new waders are like far-off dogs, whining.
My shoulder-strap could be a wheatear
turning a corner. The wind, through the cleat
of my landing-net, makes the squeaking
of many mice busying themselves under cover.
On his ledge overlooking the loch
the buzzard that is too big for a buzzard
eyes everything stonily, then takes his pick.

II

Uist, a smashed mirror.
I holiday here, to gather
strength for the winter.
So I fire my peats, gut
trout, rub cold hands together:
reassured that when December
does come, I shall be far
from here. Like all city dwellers.

III

I try to locate a tiny ratchet
at my right ear, an insomniac
cheese-grater somewhere beyond my toes.
The place is hoaching with mice. They are in
for the winter. Every so often
we have an eyeball to eyeball confrontation.
One way to dispose of them is to fire
the thatch. A costly operation.

IV

Three days I have trudged
after a pair of eagles; sighting them
occasionally, overhead or on fence-stakes,
surveying their land. This evening,

probing gobbets of fur, disgorged bone,
I am perceived by a hind who stands
sniffing, then bounds over the wire
and effortlessly away.

V

Striding back from the Co-op, I clutch
sodden groceries in a plastic bag
one handle of which is sprung.
Proud of the buffeting
I'm taking, I feel I belong:
till I meet a chained mongrel,
yap-yapping; and an old woman
who slurches past, head down.

VI

The sky consists of strips
of blue, like a holiday postcard.
I sit writing, like a man writing
a holiday postcard. The strips
turn to steel, to smoky grey.
The tide recedes, and recedes,
all the way to Vallay. Meanwhile
the multitudinous sandworms turn and turn.

VII

If, as the pundits say,
a new Ice Age does
come, well I suppose Uist
will be as ready as most.
The skuas sharp as razors;
the lochans, crystal.
And in the long chambers,
the War Lords are sleeping still.

Driving Through Sutherland

Here too the crofts were burned
to the ground, families stripped
and driven like cattle to the shore.
You can still hear the cursing,
the women shrieking.

                        The Duke
and his lady sipped port, had
wax in their ears. Thatch
blazed. Thistles were torn up
by the root.

              There are men
in Parliament today could
be doing more.

                        With these thoughts
in mind we drive from Overscaig
to Lairg, through a night as blue
as steel.

              Leaving Loch Shin behind
we find facing us an even colder
firth, and a new moon rising
delicately over a stubble field.

Summer, Assynt

(for John and Lynne Arnott)

After three weeks' rain, Drumbeg is a swampland;
Suilven's tonsured skull lost
in mist. The forecasters extend
a blessing everywhere except 'the north-west'.

Marooned cattle peer
through columns of moisture.
The lochs are less Landseer
than Japanese watercolour.

By evening, we can see
the nearer hills. Under pale skies
summer visitors emerge – like empty
vessels, shifting in the breeze.

*

Dear Lord Vestey
he had to write, *please
accept my apologies
for fishing your water
with worm*: otherwise
the ban would remain.
This after the discovery
of two cock salmon
along with his bait tin.
He gazes at anglers
in green chest-waders
casting monotonously.
Suddenly his expression
changes. Light glances
in his eyes as he sees,
through the birches,
two boys stealthily
pursuing old ways …

*

You, Loch Torr nan Hidhean
in the lee of Canisp, took some persuasion.
Loch a Braighe, you too showed a firm will
before yielding a speckled fighter from your cross-ripple.

Despite your chill, Loch Gorm Mor,
a change of fly finally got your measure.
Then on the way home
to fail with you, Lochan-of-no-Name:

naive enough to try
and outreach your pads of water-lily
I left in your dark bed an imprint deeper
than I care to remember.

                                         *

'Leave the cooker and kitchen
as you find them: clean.'
On our last afternoon, as is proper,
we eliminate any reminder

of our presence – so that whoever
should be next here
finds no cup-ring or soup-stain
but all spick and span.

As for the land around, little need
for circumspection. A neap tide
laps where we clambered
or sat pullovered –

while long before we drive away
we will trickle into anonymity;
the wader-prints round each lochan
fished, by brimming waters filled in.

At Coruisk

I

Think of it: a honeymoon at the foot
of the Cuillin, and not once to see them
for mist – till on the last day we broached
from Elgol the seven crowned kings.

So intense the experience: not summer only,
but years, cramming one afternoon –
thus keenly the glimpse awaited.
Nor had been envisaged such blueness:

ice-crests mirrored in Coruisk, blue
upon blue, as we followed
the path home. The moon crescent.
The sky, powdered flint.

II

Tempting to see these things
as manifestations of the mind
significant through ourselves,
which precede and succeed our notice.

For all that, those shadows are real.
They darken or illumine, at will;
are points from which
to examine ourselves. But watch

how you go: yonder are scurrs
would cut you down; nearer
to hand, peat-holes
where you'd cramp and drown.

III

So we get to know landscape,
and each other, better;
our breathing filling the air
with each lap tackled. We learn

that the end of a road is seldom
a fixed point; bridges exist
too narrow to be crossed
more than one abreast.

And remains the fear, when
we look round, that two figures
not dissimilar to ourselves should appear
transparent, then vanish altogether.

Marriage a Mountain Ridge

I

Like most, one way or another, ours
has been through some dark couloirs.

I cannot swear to actual crevasses –
but have sensed them underfoot. (One night

on Bheinn Fhada I lost my footing,
and was fortunate a rowan took my weight.)

That way I am better equipped
for keeping, if not to the spirit, the letter.

Crampons and pitons fitted, we face
the next assault, roped together. I also carry

an ice-pick – but fear to use it,
lest it sink too deeply in.

II

Perhaps the hardest lesson
is to accept the Brocken,

the Man with the Rainbow, as stemming
from myself; a projection

of my own form. The cauldron
below me, thin air.

In these rarified labyrinths
the way forward

is to focus
on a fixed point,

one hand firmly gripping
its moral thread.

III

Whether scaling Etive
of the shifting faces

or on the summit of Blaven,
sheet-ice glistening

through walls of mist,
it is all one. The tracks

we pursue are ours;
the zone we would enter

not the mountains, but ourselves.
So for a moment, the mind

may afford to swing out
over the wide abyss.

IV

Then comes the point when body
and mind are one, each indefinable

except in terms of the other.
Head and heart held

in a single nose. The Beast,
the Grey Man, cannot touch us here.

His footprints descending,
identical with our own.

Later, victims of Time and Loss,
we will return and gaze there –

and marvel at such heights
conquered, such blazing air.

Orkney Shore

A cormorant flew
    round the Peerie Sea
as if to say,
    this belongs to me.

But the island mists
    grew grey then white,
till the island rose
    on a ribbon of light.

The hourglass island
    webbed him in
with the scything wings
    of his own dark sin.

The treeless land
    may break back, but he
will be shell and skull
    in the Peerie Sea.

The Predators

1

From Aquitaine, its turrets and towers
yellow with age, limestone lashed
by the sun, its baked pantiles

and fig-groves, Isaiah's robe flowing
like flame; in the path
of de Montfort's sordid plunder

we rise through layer upon layer
of spiders-webs white in the mist;
by train, follow the gorge

(lines forged in red rock),
then by bus track the causse
toward Conques. The last miles on foot.

2

As, parched and footsore, pilgrims
for Compostella climbed to the spring,
fed and huddled in the clerestory for warmth:

who in times past had left no alms –
till a brother purloined from a nearby
abbey the relics of Ste Foy.

Thereafter, the church built. Cool
cloisters, the fountains stuffed with pike,
a vault in clue course added

to the tympanum with its carved
angels and devils, eyes
pierced, a Last Judgment in stone.

3

During the Revolution the church treasure
divided for safe keeping among
the peasants; later gathered in, no item

missing.
      Including the great cross,
tapestries depicting the Saint's
decapitation at the hands

of the Romans.
      Also her likeness
in beaten gold, enthroned and bedizened
with intaglios from the faithful (penitents

and others) – Marcus Aurelius
in agate; Aeneas, the deepest
jade; Caligula all jowls and curls.

4

Yet the treasure unseemly
under its glass case. Nothing prim
in the mouth (as most Saints)

but a hard line. The blue eyes, enamel.
Barbaric, that the relics of a child
should have lain within this cocoon.

In the church, dust drifts.
The choir-rails are spiked.
Here too the spiders are at work.

The pulpit is meshed in web. High
overhead a bird that has flown in
beats silently from beam to beam.

5

Outside, on a hill track,
I reach a mica-ridge: coil
of flesh to tilt of bone.

Three huntsmen pass a station
of the cross. Their barrels
flash; the rabbits' heads

swell. Here 'were rounded up
and set before a firing-squad
in the public square (by way

of reprisal) all members
of the local Resistance, June '44' –
having been first betrayed.

6

Much earlier, the impact of Rome:
Caesar persuading the Gauls
their gods had abandoned them

and, for delaying his conquest,
having the right hand of each male
struck off.
        Under Dacian

the martyrdom for her faith
of Ste Foy.
        Since when the wheel
has turned: the slit corpses

of Protestants choking the well
at Penne; Coligny himself
exacting the most atrocious revenge.

7

Notwithstanding, the church
faces the chestnut slopes,
the vineyards beyond. Human vice depicted

in sculpted stone. At the centre,
that idol in gold. A lay-brother
leads crowds of tourists

from the garth. In the nave
all is silent. My eyes
are drawn up and up. Layers

of light stream through the vault.
The bird beats itself senseless
against the stone. Below, the webs wait.

III

The Lilypond

I stand at the edge of the lilypond
with its swart fronds
and submerged stems. Scarcely defined
forms nudge the surface and dip back down.

Years ago, I remember, the water
was clear; the leaves green saucers
you wanted to walk on. Beyond,
the hot-house. Now its spars

are smashed, the iron flamingoes
gone. One day too, the pond
is to be drained. I shall not be here.
Better simply arrive and find

the area filled in, than see
the process as I imagine it:
orange shapes with white
growths being scooped out

by men in rubber gloves,
then speedily disposed of.
I'd be free to surmise
the stench, the bunches of flies.

In so many ways, we avoid
being in at the death;
letting nature take its course,
and putting in an appearance

when we know all is safe.
Again and again I am drawn
here, to the lilypond.
Elsewhere, there is hurt enough.

Kilchrenan

Looking out on Cruachan, the church is whitewashed;
monuments to McIntyre and McCorquedale

kept simple, Cailean Mor's sword set in stone.
The old days would see some cold funerals.

As always the gentry dominate. Two lofts
used to face each other, where the lairds

sat crossing glances, smouldering slowly
under their ordered curls... the sermon droning.

See them descend, their ladies in lace,
then jog arrogantly off, leaving behind

an odour of musk and Madeira, where now sheep
go blindly nudging clumps of daffodils.

A Sense of Order

Sunday walk

I stop at the foot of Garioch Drive
where my aunt used to live
three floors up.
    I remember the smell
of camomile that hit you in the hall,
the embroidered sampler, the jars
of wax chrysanths, the budgerigars
in their lacquered cage; the ladies who came
to read the Bible in the front room –
surrounded by marzipan, and dragons
on silky screens.

A rag-and-bone man,
his pony ready for the knacker's yard,
rounds a corner (short of a tail light)
and disappears up Clouston Street.

Below, the Kelvin runs like stinking lard.

Period piece

Hand in hand, the girls glide
along Great Western Road.
            Outside
the Silver Slipper the boys wait,
trousers flared, jacket-pockets
bulging with carry-outs.

The girls approach. A redhead
pouts, sticks her tongue out,
then passes under the strung lights
to the dance-floor. 'I'll have it
off with that one.' 'Wanna bet?'
'I'd rather lumber her mate...'

They nick their cigarettes.
            Inside,
the miniskirts are on parade,
listening to The Marmalade.

Cranworth Street

I climb the tenement stair
with its scoured tiles, odour
of cat.
    We lived here, before
moving to Ayrshire.
I have not been back, for years.

The brass nameplate, the square
bellpull, mean nothing any more.
What is there to recapture,
to rediscover?

                Too late
in the season, for that.

I cling to the wooden
rail and for no reason
break out in a sweat
as I reach the street.

Street scene

The faces outside the Curlers
explode like fat cigars
in the frosty air.

Even the newsvendor
rocks on his heels, half-seas over.
And I don't blame him.

As the pictures
come out, scores of lovers
head for their parked cars.

Two ladies whisper
goodnight to each other.
Neither feels secure

till on her own stair
she snibs the basement door
and breathes freely, behind iron bars.

Portents

Southpark

The area palls, and its mildewed parades.
　　Victorian terraces,
　taken over for the University, lose
their ironwork, their fluted balustrades.

Among the charred bedsteads, the crazy mirrors,
　　I keep thinking of those men in dungarees
　putting an axe through Mackintosh's
front door... Glasgow is in arrears.

The salon

The supporting programme always began
at 5.30. But they didn't open
　　till 5.28. So that
　by the time you'd got your ticket
　　and found your seat
you'd missed the first four minutes.

Once when we could scarcely see the screen
　for fog, we didn't complain –
　but sat through the entire programme again.
　Phantom cops, after a phantom Keaton.

　In December, the gate
　was locked. The white
frontage peels. The posters are gone
but for a clutch of curls, a crimped grin.

Costume piece

Every morning two women in Edwardian costume
stood for hours opposite the men's Union.
It seemed one or other had been let down
by a medical student: clear water over sharp stones.
When they disappeared, we hoped for a happy
conclusion – only to hear both had been put away.

Botanics

Somewhere, a clock strikes. Schoolboys
   in cherry caps and corduroys
face the death-trap of Great Western Road
   watched by a lollipop-man, then head

for the ice-cream parlour
   and the Gardens – where the keeper,
not wanting trouble, goes inside
   to his prize orchids, his marble nudes.

Behind the hothouse the boys shout
   at an artist in sombrero and tights
too dour even to look up. By the gate
   the winnowing fantails preen and pirouette.

After the Party

I drive you home, your seat-belt fastened
to take you in. Your time draws near. Never

have I seen on you such a bloom. Fears skim
the surface. Most remain unspoken. Now

and again though, we talk the next stage through.
The car garaged, I follow you in. Loaded with gifts

we've been given. Who survive by moving
from one house of glass to another.

Family Visit

Laying linoleum, my father spends hours
with his tape-measure
littering the floor
as he checks his figures, gets
the angle right; then cuts
carefully, to the music
of a slow logic. In despair
I conjure up a room where
a boy sits and plays with coloured bricks.

My mind tugging at its traces,
I see him in more dapper days
outside the Kibble Palace
with my grandfather, having
his snapshot taken; men firing
that year's leaves.
The Gardens are only a stone's throw
from where I live ... But now
a younger self comes clutching at my sleeve.

Or off to Innellan, singing, we would go,
boarding the steamer at the Broomielaw
in broad summer, these boomps-a-daisy
days, the ship's band playing in a lazy
swell, my father steering well clear
of the bar, mother making neat
packets of waste-paper to carry
to the nearest basket or (more likely)
all the way back to Cranworth Street.

Leaving my father at it
(he'd rather be alone) I take
my mother through the changed Botanics.
The bandstand is gone, and the great
rain-barrels that used to rot
and overflow. Everything is neat
and plastic. And it is I who must walk
slowly for her, past the sludge
and pocked granite of Queen Margaret Bridge.

To My Father

One of my earliest memories (remember
those Capone hats, the polka-dot ties)
is of the late thirties: posing
with yourself and grandfather before
the park railings; me dribbling

ice-cream, you so spick and smiling
the congregation never imagined
how little you made. Three generations,
in the palm of a hand. A year later
grandfather died. War was declared.

In '42 we motored to Kilmarnock
in Alec Martin's Terraplane Hudson.
We found a pond, and five goldfish
blurred under ice. They survived
that winter, but a gull got them in the end.

Each year we picnicked on the lawn;
mother crooking her finger
as she sipped her lime. When
they carried you out on a stretcher
she knew you'd never preach again.

Since you retired, we've seen more
of each other. Yet I spend this forenoon
typing, to bring you closer – when
we might have been together. Part of what
I dread is that clear mind nodding

before its flickering screen. If we come over
tonight, there will be the added irony
of proving my visit isn't out of duty
when, to myself, I doubt the dignity
of a love comprising so much guilt and pity.

Reawakening

'Worse than that, the walls smeared
with excrement, adults with the minds
of children, behaving like pigs
at a trough; men circling the yard,
each with a hand on the shoulder
of the man in front. One patient
kept in a padded cell, lest he rape
someone as he did his mother
in '24: the face frozen, body slow
but for the hands' constant fever.'

My father has not broached the subject
of his thesis, *encephalitis lethargica*,
for as long as I can remember. Today
I show him an article in *The Listener*
describing how a new drug has awakened
a group of patients in the States: one woman
paralysed forty years leapt to her feet,
ran round the ward, shattered inmate
and doctor alike – then had to face
being two ages, at the same time.

'Most frightening, the moral decay:
one female student caught the disease
(this confirming its infectious nature)
and soon had the University in a turmoil.
How she ended up, I couldn't say...
Thanks for underlining those sections,
that helps ... The strongest argument I've known
for euthanasia: the wrong side
of the story of the Sleeping Beauty,
no cure known, least of all a kiss.'

Putting the paper aside, he tells
of the research he did; using expressions
he must have thought he'd forgotten;
referring to a thesis that has lain
in a drawer for thirty years:
his mind awakening, at the one time,
to what he did – and what he might have done.

In the Kibble Palace

In the Kibble Palace with its dazzling statues
and glass dome, reading a poet I've just come across,
I learn that under ice the killer whale

seeing anything darker than snow, falls away
then charges, smashing the ice with his forehead,
to isolate seal or man on a drifting piece

of the floe. Imagine those tons of blubber
thrusting up; tail curveting
as the hammer head hits. What if the skull

should split, splinters penetrate to the brain?
Nor will dry land protect us from the thudding
in the blood, those forces below. How can we conquer

who cannot conquer ourselves? I shall think of this
when, fishing on frosted glass, I find
my line tightening against the swell;

or hearing you moan and turn in your sleep
I know you are on your own, far out,
dark shapes coursing below. Meanwhile

the horizon closes in, a glass
globe. We will admit it is there
when it is too late; and blunder for the exits

to find them locked. Seeing as though through ice
blurred forms gyrate, we will put our heads
together and try to batter a way out.

Tremors

We took turns at laying
an ear on the rail –
so that we could tell
by the vibrations

when a train was coming.
Then we'd flatten ourselves
to the banks, scorched
vetch and hedge-parsley,

while the iron flanks
rushed past, sending sparks
flying. It is more and more
a question of living

with an ear to the ground:
the tremors, when they come,
are that much greater –
for ourselves and others.

Nor is it any longer
a game, but a matter
of survival: each explosion
part of a procession

there can be no stopping.
Though the end is known,
there is nothing for it
but to keep listening …

Before Dark

(for Douglas Dunn)

They are so confident, the young, who strut
    through the avenues that once were ours;
    so sure of themselves, knowing the future is theirs;
so cool and relaxed, as they scale the sweet
    octaves of love; so self-possessed,
    desire not yet on the wane, or become lust.

A bell sounds. The end of lectures for today.
    They fan out across the pastures
    of the city, filling the nearest bars
or returning to bed-sitters, wearily.
    The old smells linger: in Gibson Street,
    curry powder; stale urine, from the Pewter Pot.

In my mind it will always be winter
    in this Victorian sector of the city,
    its terraces squandered by the University,
heaped with swept leaves, a rotting umber;
    Kelvingrove a vast litter-bin; children
    playing, generation upon generation.

I still have black and white snapshots taken
    in front of wrought-iron gates, in the early
    days of the War; my father wearing a kipper tie.
How long I wonder, before our children,
    asked who we were, explain idly if lovingly?
    In old age perhaps the rarest quality –

certainly the one I most envy – is dignity,
    especially in the face of pain. I cannot bear
    the thought of what loved-ones may suffer.
This is partly what drives me to poetry.
    The Missa Solemnis on, we sit and listen:
    From the heart, may it go to the heart again.

Arrivals

I

The plane meets
its reflection on the wet
runway, then crosses
to where I wait
behind plate glass.

I watch
with a mixture
of longing and despair
as you re-enter
the real world.

All we have is each other.
I sometimes wonder
if that is enough;
whether being together
enlarges or diminishes grief.

II

Remember arriving
from Thorame –
the scent
of honey
of lavender clinging.

On the Jonte,
climbing goat-tracks
to drink from a spring
under an arch
of red sandstone.

Or last year,
a second honeymoon
in Amsterdam, having
exchanged gifts: a miniature
war-horse, a silver ring.

III

Tonight your return
from Ulster
renders my fears
unfounded.
Yet neither

of us speaks. Instead
we think of those
living there, others
who have died.
Your brother-in-law

has decided to emigrate:
the one sure escape.
As I draw up
at the lights, you droop
forward, hands on your lap.

IV

The pubs are coming out.
In Dumbarton Road
two drunks, having battered
each other senseless, sit
in their own vomit.

No one interferes.
It is not easy
to accept there may
be a certain mercy
in living here.

The lights turn
to green. I imagine
you lying alone
in a white room, surrounded
by flimsy screens...

Witnesses

Jehovah's witnesses have been, and gone,
their steel rims flashing in the sun.
Some sixth sense warned me to remain
under cover, till I had seen

who was at the door. They were
persuasive as ever: 'Prepare
to act on the good news.' 'Can you envisage
a future without God?' 'It is our privilege

to invite you to partake of His banquet...'
Our upstairs neighbour, firm but discreet,
closes the door. Father of two young children,
mine is a different desperation.

I sit tight in my sense of sin.
Their dark figures diminish, in the sun.

Two Poems

Night incident

Three nights running
you have wakened crying:

this time, because you heard
footsteps in your bedroom cupboard.

How do I help you understand
beyond

saying they are
from next door?

You calm down,
ask to see the moon.

It is full, tonight.
As we look out

I think of a lifetime
of haunted rooms,

of the violence
that is your inheritance.

I carry
you carefully

upstairs, and put
you in your cot;

then tiptoe to the door.
Your breathing is there, and no more.

Ghosts

My face against the bars
of your cot, close to yours,

I listen while you whisper
urgently, telling me where

you want to go. Needless
to say, it is the Kibble Palace.

As soon as you are dressed
and have had breakfast

we set off; a fine
mist rising from the Kelvin.

We are alone in the Gardens.
Leaving the pram at the entrance

I take you to where the goldfish are.
For what seems hours, you peer

through the murky
water. Under the lattice-work

of white spars, whose
curved glass has

mirrored family upon family,
we too shall soon be,

like my father and grandfather,
ghosts in the empty air.

Seize the Day

Come on Daddy, come now I hear them shout
as I put the finishing touches to this and that

in the safe confines of my study:
Hurry daddy before it's too late, we're ready!

They are so right. Now is the time.
It won't wait, on that you can bet your bottom

dollar. So rouse yourself, get the drift
before you're muffled and left

for useless. *Let's build a snowman, then
a snow-woman to keep him company. When*

*that's finished, and with what's left over,
a giant snow-ball that will last for ever,*

only hurry daddy. As soon as this poem
is finished, I promise, I'll come –

essential first, to pin down what is felt.
Meanwhile the snow begins to melt.

Return Visit

Revisiting the Kibble Palace
after years of absence
is once more to witness
time's destructiveness.

The statues have lost
their piercing whiteness.
The herbage is less dense.
Even the glass dome seems

diminished in circumference.
To think my grandfather
carried me here; my sons in turn
scouring this pool for goldfish

and silted coins.
Now the lilies have gone.
And look how tawdry
the entrance has become.

When we leave, we cross
the shrunken Gardens,
not glancing behind us.
Later, at a distance,

I concede that what's lost
is within myself: the past
cannot be repossessed.
What future there is, is theirs.

IV

Under the Ice

Like Coleridge, I waltz
on ice. And watch my shadow
on the water below. Knowing that
if the ice were not there
I'd drown. Half willing it.

In my cord jacket
and neat cravat, I keep
returning to the one spot.
How long, to cut
a perfect circle out?

Something in me
rejects the notion.
The arc is never complete.
My figures-of-eight
almost, not quite, meet.

Was Raeburn's skating parson
a man of God, poised
impeccably on the brink;
or his bland stare
no more than a decorous front?

If I could keep my cool
like that. Gazing straight ahead,
not at my feet. Giving
no sign of knowing
how deep the water, how thin the ice.

Behind that, the other
question: whether the real you
pirouettes in space,
or beckons from under the ice
for me to come through.

In the Gallery

SCOTTISH NATIONAL GALLERY, EDINBURGH

(for Marilyn and James Runcie)

Heading for the National Gallery
to renew acquaintance with the Turner watercolours
I find I am formulating an analogy
between this aesthetic pleasure and the urgency
with which we must face fierce

mortality. For one month only of each year
are these paintings on display,
lest their colours
succumb to the light's rays.
So in marriage, we must seize

every opportunity to act lovingly,
while fire is kept at bay. May
God in his mercy let us share
a little longer the charmed lives we bear.
So I make for these subtle blues and ochres,

illustrations on smooth-grained paper
of weightless lakes and rivers; trees
like plumes, waterfalls suspended in mid-air;
on the bank, tiny transient figures –
only when I get there to discover

today is the first of February.
Accepting this as salutary, I take away
in my mind's eye a graver imagery:
Rembrandt, ageing; and Goya's doctor,
heating his hands under a wintry sky.

Kitchen Maid

Reaching the Rijksmuseum
mid-morning, in rain,
we skirt the main hall
with its tanned
tourists and guides

and, ignoring the rooms
we saw yesterday,
find ourselves heading
past Avercamp's skaters,
Brueghel's masses of flowers

and even the Night-Watch
in its noisy arena
till, up carpeted stairs,
we are in a chamber
made cool by Vermeer.

For what might be hours
we stand facing
a girl in a blue apron
pouring milk
from a brown jug.

Time comes to a stop.
her gesture will stay
perpetually in place.
The jug will never empty,
the bowl never fill.

It is like seeing
a princess
asleep, under ice.
Your hand, brushing mine,
sustains the spell:

as I turn to kiss you,
we are ourselves
suspended in space;
your appraising glance
a passionate embrace.

Visiting Hour

In the pond of our new garden
were five orange stains, under
inches of ice. Weeks since anyone
had been there. Already by far
the most severe winter for years.
You broke the ice with a hammer.
I watched the goldfish appear,
blunt-nosed and delicately clear.

Since then so much has taken place
to distance us from what we were.
That it should have come to this.
Unable to hide the horror
in my eyes, I stand helpless
by your bedside and can do no more
than wish it were simply a matter
of smashing the ice and giving you air.

Afternoon Visit

It is a gusty April afternoon.
    The wrestling is on television,
punctuated by adverts. Her walking, even
    this past week, has slowed down

perceptibly, her leg grown stiffer.
    At one point, getting up
to adjust the set, she overbalances. Before
    either of us can intervene, a cup

and saucer fall to the floor.
    Neither breaks. What does snap,
surprisingly, is her composure.
    Taking her grandchild on her lap

she strokes his head over and over again,
　　not noticing the tears
flow. 'Love is the main
　　thing. Yet let Nature take its course.

Children are their own. Time must come,
　　it cannot be helped.' And strokes
that helpless head. I remember at home
　　sitting on her lap, surrounded by books

and ornaments bought over the years,
　　most of them to be chipped, at least,
by ourselves as children. 'There's
　　no evading it ...' Some fearful beast

within me refuses to listen; would smash
　　down the walls, the watercolours
in their frames, the precious trash
　　of a lifetime. I am no longer hers,

she is saying – not knowing it
　　but speaking simply, without grievance,
from the heart. How can I be fit
　　to raise children, I wonder; tense

with foreboding on their behalf and my own,
　　who am already a father before
having learned to be a son.
　　The child slips to the floor

and plays there. Her eyes mist
　　over. I concentrate on the faded green
of an apron. What will become of us, at the last?
　　Men fight through blizzards, on the TV screen.

Snowman

Overnight, the thaw came.
All trace of snow had gone
from the gardens. Yet
when I looked out, what
should I see but a snowman
in the middle of the lawn.
I thought of Wallace Stevens'
nothing that is not there
and the nothing that is
and decided to try again
with my glasses on. Sure
enough it was there still,
large as ... well, life. No one
near, or looking even.

Was it a crystallisation
of guilt and desire,
this conjunction of elements
customarily hidden?
Adjusting focus, I realise
it is some object
wrapped in white polythene.
Before there is a chance
to explore further
a man from next door
hoists it on his shoulder
and carries it in; leaving
only a nagging circle
on the grass where it had been.

Snowfall

Slabs of snow, stacked against the guttering,
keel on the lip, then slop down
on the tarred tubs littering
the area. Each clearance brings
filthy water, as from a gushet;
a juddering of blocked veins.
We switch off television, sit
watching nothing. Each of us wonders what
to say. Tomorrow we shall have the great
thaw to discuss. Meanwhile there is tonight.

*

'Like felled logs,' you say. And 'Yes, the alarm
has gone, did you not hear?' A small child charms
us with, 'Open the shutters, so I can see out.'
The mind wallowing from last night's
trough, I go through. The rutted snow
has gone to slush, not frozen. Along the Row
cars start. People pass, looking in.
I switch off the centre-light. Our bin
is on the pavement, on its side,
its lid gone. Is there nothing we can hide?

*

They are bringing the dead off the mountain.
It has been the worst winter for years.
You ask, can we go sledging. In the Gardens
yesterday a father sat his small daughter,
shrieking with laughter, on a new toboggan,
then watched helpless as it careered
downhill into a tree. I still hear
the crack of her skull – and cannot tear
myself from this glazed Japanese
bowl, its surface minutely crazed.

At the Airport

We wave goodbye and watch them go,
loved and familiar figures, through
the security check, and on. In next to no
time, they will descend on Ulster,

a charred land I lay no claim to
other than through them, my parents-in-law.
They used to go by steamer from the Broomielaw;
later, the shorter journey from Stranraer

to Larne. Now the journey is more speedy,
but the gulf between us and the greenery
of Down and Antrim grown immeasurably –
so that what I see when people say

'Get the Army out' are two elderly
heads on a pillow, steeped in blood. To me
if not to most, politics are secondary
to the tug of personal loyalty.

On the periphery of our lives
as they now are of ours,
we will be over the water
when our children are older,

who already have privacies
we cannot share... So much
of life is a biting back of fear.
Their plane is a speck in cerulean skies.

Lothian Burn

Up here, scarcely
birdsong even: only

the labials and gutturals
of this burn as it gurgles

downhill, locality of accent
in vowel and consonant,

each circumlocution
through heather and sandstone

traced by inflection
and sharp interjection

until, in a mossy outcrop,
it comes to a glottal stop.

Moving In

October ends. Against my study wall
the rose-hips shrivel. The central

heating is like leaves shifting
behind the skirting. The boys'

woollens and long stockings
are laid out for the morning.

Since the hour went back
there has been mist, incessant rain.

At dusk the New Town
comes into its own:

a cat at each corner, shady permutations
of wives and lovers gliding through its lanes.

In bed, we cling to one another
and prepare for a long winter.

Offshore

Edging from shingle, the dinghy turns
   a tight half-circle, heading past the island
with its twisted pines, the twin horns
   of rock guarding the bay, out across the sound.

Opposite the lighthouse we ship the oars
   and drift, lopsided. The boys let out handlines,
each hook hidden in plastic and red feathers:
   preferable, they feel, to bait moiling in tins.

Each, thinking he has a bite, finds weed.
   Small hands grow icier, with each haul;
until only hope deferred, and pride,
   sustain them. I wish them mackerel –

but find my thoughts turn, coldly, towards
   the foreign fleets who come
trawling our shores; recalling the words
   of those who say this was a fisherman's kingdom

once, the surface phosphorescent from shoals
   of herring feeding; holds crammed,
decks silver with their scales,
   a bygone age, not likely to return; the unnamed,

as is customary, having destroyed. The boys,
   eyes glistening with weariness and trepidation,
wind in for the last time. Grown wise,
   they know I know there's nothing on the line.

End of Season, Drumelzier

Scarcely discernible, the line tautens
against the current, then sweeps downstream.
The rod-tip shifts, dislodging a thin
gleam of light. I spool in, cast again.

So the season ends. In near darkness
I try to reach the rise.
Something jumps. The circles
are absorbed. Night closes in.

I stumble from the luminescent Tweed
and trudge by torchlight to the farm,
then home: waders discarded, I concentrate
on the winding road; watch hedgerows pass,

sheer banks; branches like weed, overhead.
Sedgeflies smudge the screen. I bear left
towards row upon row of lights that never meet.
In under an hour, I am crossing Princes Street.

So the close of each trout season
brings its own desperation
to make up for lost days; a trek
to the river, a casting more frantic

than judged. In life and love too, take care
to make the most of time – before,
darkness encroaching, it is too late
for anything but the final onslaught.

Cherry Tree, at Dusk

The gales have, this past week,
been worse than at the equinox;
leaves spiralling, as though
caught in a thermal; the main bough

of next door's sycamore crazily
overhanging. Through it all, amazingly,
the blossom has clung on:
each bloom, a tiny beacon.

Bedtime Story

'I don't like that one, Hansel
and Gretel, I told them so, little
children enticed by a wicked witch
into her marzipan cottage – such
goings-on – too fearsome
for words, just before bedtime
too: keep them up half the night.'

They recognise her plight,
interpret it differently:
Grandma would be upset, you see
they confide later, from tact:
It's the old woman who gets cooked.

The Eye-shade

Finding this eye-shade on the kitchen table
and putting it on, I am able

for the first time to counteract the glare
from the desk-light in my study. Your father

wore it latterly, to protect failing eyesight.
Now in minute part, I can inhabit

his world, gauge its curve, grow sensitive
to its more manageable perspective.

His spectrum we knew had been restricted,
his Emerald Isle made more so, as predicted –

each image on his television screen,
not only grass and baize, reduced to green.

The eye-shade would have been appropriate
if earlier he could have worn it

when burning the midnight oil, as editor
of the Abbey's monthly newsletter.

Truly, what intervening object can impede
the vision of the good? Nor can his shade

do us harm, if it focuses the mind on others
or induces an old age in which like him we conquer,

with verve and humour, bereavement and despair:
a lovely man, most distant yet most dear.

Recovery

(for Iain Crichton Smith)

I

You know now 'what inhuman pressures
keep a line of verse
on its own course'. The everlasting flowers
shiver in their vase.

And you in a strange place
believing your loved ones
have turned against you.
Behind incandescent mirrors

to be imprisoned...
All I can do is will you
patience and reassurance
and through them, peace of mind.

II

The poet's task, to seek
significant detail
in the face of horror.

It has always been so –
Yeats and Marvell writing
out of disturbance and war.

Like preserving a journal
through plague years.
And consider the chill

chambers, now ruined,
where were produced
those beautiful Books of Hours.

III

Or do you see yourself as Hamlet
in black, on black battlements waiting?
Do you hear the ghost clanking,
the jewelled clock within you, ticking?

Mercifully things are more mundane
on this side of the mirror – no one
plotting to kill you, no cup of poison,
no revenge tragedy, no treacherous queen.

If only the trees outside your window,
bristling with weaponry, could revert
to an uncomplicated green; the tides
off Oban sparkle, as they used to.

IV

It must have been
like winter closing in,
the mind an icy
web; in your case

a sea-loch,
its surface
seeming to freeze
yet retaining

the intellect's finery
and pulsing beneath,
those massive forces,
endurance and love.

At Amersham

(for Kay)

I

Entering the chapel, you survey
for a moment your husband's coffin.
He's gone, after an illness
made less hideous by the devotion
shown in its face. Your coat is green,
his colour. On your wedding-finger
the matching ring from Amsterdam,
where you spent your honeymoon
two years ago. There comes a kind of trembling.
Like a young bride, you walk down
the aisle. The lovelorn bouquets loom.

II

The curtain is closed, the benediction
said. We come out, into the sun.

Your black limousine accelerates down the drive.
Grief is poised in the air, the crest of a wave.

III

In my mind's eye, I see a stretch
of bare beach; on it, the wind
howling, a reed that bends –
and will not snap.

In Monte Mario

I lie staring at the ceiling, unable to sleep.
In the room opposite, surrounded by scalpels
and glass-topped bottles, Ettore restores lovingly
a Bassano landscape clamped to its easel.
Over my bed, in an oval frame, gilt but unadorned,
is a sensuous Madonna ascribed to Leonardo:
the same model as his Virgin
of the Rocks; the tilt of her chin
caught on canvas at the time of the Borgias;
surveying this room, in a Rome torn by explosion;
even in darkness, radiating tenderness.

Her presence makes me more tense than were any
woman of flesh beside me. Each time I stretch
for the light-switch, a single mosquito
settles just out of reach. At last I rise
and tiptoe murderously across the room –
to be drawn back to her portrait. So
exquisite the dilemma: the wiry creature
perches precisely on the nose of the Madonna.

Springtime

In front of me a girl with bare feet,
in a beribboned dress, picks white
flowers in a field somewhere near Pompeii.

Each day I look at her, head straight,
right hand outstretched as she delicately
plucks the stem. Was she there that night

the lava flowed, birds shrivelled in the sky
and lovers turned to ash, where they lay?
If so, what had she done to deserve it?

I wonder, will it ever be
springtime again, the blood flow freely?
Or has man blighted all hope of recovery?

We are on borrowed time, you and I,
and have been from the outset.
All that is left, is to live lovingly.

V

The Luncheon of the Boating Party

I *Alphonse*

'Have you nothing better to do?', calls
my father, not discreetly, as would befit
my station (son of the proprietor, after all)
but in a blacksmith's bellow, spittle flecking
his chin: 'These boats need repairing.' Instead

I lean on the balustrade, observer and observed,
posing for a painting. (When will he understand
it is not seemly to move, once positioned?)
By an artisan too, no mistake about it:
a true painter who finds the term *artist* effete.

How long it could take, God knows. Some *cocotte*
wrote asking to be in it. When she found Angèle
already here, the fur flew. 'Snotty bitch!'
'Just because you sat for Degas!' From our upper terrace
come their voices, across four decades.

And all illusion: the fourteen of us
never together at the one time, far less
spaciously composed. That aside, why make me
so severe, and Caillebotte, seated opposite,
conspicuously fresh-faced? Not that I'm other

than proud to be there: look how many (a Baron
included) it took to counterbalance me.
Most astounding, the light: no criss-cross of shade
under the striped awning, but a steady suffusion.
The way he depicts it forces me to re-remember.

'That must be the boatman,' I suddenly overhear,
'waiting till luncheon's over, to ply his trade.'
'Or Charon, envisaging the placing of coins,
in due time.' Not dreaming I'd catch the reference,
or realising how, uppermost in my mind

and complementing those succulent flesh-tones,
was Renoir's skin, even then tightening on his bones
like canvas stretched over the frame of a painting;
as in one of those pleasure-boats, long-since gone,
he would sit, to be rowed across the dappled Seine.

II *The Baron*

Why should he complain? What about me?
The back of my head's about all you see,
precious little else. Whereas if he'd chosen,
Renoir my dear old pal, to survey the scene
from the other end of the terrace, I'd have been

smack in the centre. With his back to the Seine.
Then he could have called his painting
Baron Barbier, cavalry officer and bohemian,
lunching with friends at the Restaurant Fournaise:
if I'd been presented full phiz, that is,

not in this retiring fashion. Between you and me
I was in fact facing him, when he began. Only
to let myself be distracted by that 'unknown
model' (the catalogue calls her) leaning over
the balustrade, ogling in my direction.

Actually her name was Maxine. I could fill you in
more fully, if you want, but don't see why
I should do her any favours when she did me none.
There she is, a nonentity preserved for posterity,
whereas I am virtually relegated to 'Anon'.

And in one of the finest paintings ever painted,
it would seem. Not that anyone dreamed that
at the time. Indeed when the moment came
to cough up, Monsieur Balensi (it seems) reneged
on the deal. I thought she was egging me on

(Maxine, that is) but it turned out all she was after
was what she could glean about my friend Maupassant.
As for that haughty buffoon, the proprietor's son
(back to him again) let me tell you something.
He was damn near not even in the picture. Renoir

painted him out, then in again, after asking him
to take off his jacket and wear a white singlet.
Do you know why? In order to highlight
the flowers on a straw hat. As though we existed
purely for his still life. What do you make of that!

III *Unknown man*

'Out there,' they said, 'on the terrace –
you're wanted.' Hearing the din
I assumed it was those oarsmen again,
kicking up a shindig. Not a bit of it –
there were some of the regulars

and a man with a pointy beard,
painting them. 'That's perfect,' he said,
'don't worry about your arms, so long
as you face in this direction.' I was only
a bit player, I realise. All the same

it was fun, to be one of them.
I well remember the conversation –
even the chaps whispering smutty jokes
to the girl with black gloves.
At one stage she covered her ears

from embarrassment. I could tell
they were both trying to get off
with her. But Renoir made it look
as though she was straightening her hat.
Such a pure spirit, to go through life

confronted by all those nudes –
complete waste, ask me. Mind you
he did, even then, have a crush
on the girl with flowers in her hat
and married her later, I gather.

Anyway, we were simply a job-lot
transformed by his painting. One laugh:
as fast as the wine went down,
his brush replenished it – Art
can't get more practical, than that.

As for the fellow in the top-hat,
I couldn't make out a word
he said. Might have been
from another planet. Mind you,
it was a magical afternoon.

IV *Madame Renoir*

Curiously enough, seeing that painting again
awakens in me not visuals so much as fragrances:
the bouquet of red wine, those grapes and peaches
in the dish under my nose; Alphonse's breath
from over my shoulder, as he munches garlic;

and the mustiness of that stupid little dog
Renoir made me hold: I'm sure it gave me fleas.
Maggiolo poured wine down its throat
for a joke – not expecting it to get its own back
which it did, biting his finger to the bone.

It must have been all in his head, from the start.
Not that you'd have known. Empty glasses and litter
everywhere; the clash of cutlery, bottles quivering...
Oh yes – the women's perfume, that comes back;
Angèle's lily-of-the-valley, something of the sort;

Ellen's sultry and spicy, like bruised fruit.
I wore rose-water, which I knew Renoir fancied.
'It makes a unity of the senses,' he said,
'with the flowers adorning your hat;
symbol of maidenhood.' I was naive enough

to believe him, I think. How ironic,
to be preserved on canvas, in full bloom,
while the body fails – most of all that
of our creator; hands deformed, the brush
strapped to his wrist with bandages

that he might paint. A whole world has gone,
never to return. Including those luxurious
days at Chatou. He always worked from the heart;
gave more than he took. Despite what they say
about him not paying his models: why should he,

when he was making them eternal?
As for me, that time is best recaptured
when I sit beside him in his wicker chair
and sense in his eyes – despite the pain –
a loving tenacity; light glancing on water.

V *Renoir*

Coarse blotches, suggestive of putrescent flesh,
was how they described my *'impressions'*
in those early days. No wonder every so often
Monet and I to escape would stuff ourselves
with larded turkey, washed down with Chambertin.

They protested, 'How can we go by other
than what is seen?' Oblivious
(so much for their breadth of vision)
that the eye ultimately sees
not through itself, but by some other thing.

(What shame anyway, in feasting heart *and* eye?)
Further irony, in my never contriving to be
the revolutionary they would have preferred.
My dream of harmony, not anarchy, all those years
I tried simply to mirror nature, to give joy.

Then there were those who in my intoxication
with female flesh saw an unbridled passion
mirroring some lust of their own – whereas
detecting in breasts and buttocks a purity as well
as beauty, I caressed with brush-strokes alone.

Their trouble, that they allow only one shade
of black, to indulge their curdled spirits.
Ignoring the shadowy blues and greens
which delight the senses, they deride red's redness;
any notion of colour sounding like a bell.

In years to come, carping critics forgotten,
my portraits will sing of Angèle and Ellen,
Gabrielle and Suzanne. If nothing else,
I will have preserved them on canvas: my strength,
and weakness. Meantime, my beloved already gone,

I find it difficult to recollect those days.
Lying twisted under this wire contraption,
I watch the bones work their way through my skin.
Soon, I shall be beyond pain. All labour done,
there will be no paints to mix, no brushes to clean.

[Les Collettes, 1991]

Renoir in Orkney

Monet might have made himself at home
among these flat, green islands
like giant water-lilies. Cézanne even,
with cliff-faces all cones and cylinders.

Not that my vision is impaired –
more a narrowing of the spectrum
to a harmony of glistening silk
as if too much light were being let in,

but without the embracing warmth
to which I am accustomed: seascape
and skyscape, a constant radiance.
It would need the skin of the place

to burst a blood vessel, or myself
to stab at it with a palette knife:
then there'd be something I could express.
Only this morning the world disappeared;

the boat I was in surrounded
by quicksilver, the bordering land
erased in mist. Like a composer
frantic for some variation

beyond a single high-pitched note
sustained in his brain,
I crave a cacophony of colour,
before my mind disintegrates.

At least with the fisherman
I am at home. Their tanned features
merit the mixing of pigments:
my yellows and reds are in business again.

As for the womenfolk, baiting the line
has made their fingers like my own
and worse: knife-gashes to the bone...
Nudes are out. For one thing, their

Kirk concedes no such tradition.
For another, contemplate the climate.
But something in me burns. I must
start again. I have found a girl

with skin like mother-of-pearl;
am working on still lives of lobsters;
and will distribute at the solstice
canvases of wild flowers, like mottled flame.

Burial Mound

Entering Maeshowe we have to bend double
for the narrow passage which brings us
to the main chamber, in whose recesses
lodged the bones and ashes
of the dead. Torch flitting from ceiling to wall

my guide recites the history of the place,
revealing chiselled runes
on slate slabs, before the beam moves on.
Hesitantly I ask, please could she
cast light again on the inscriptions:

Ingibiorg is the fairest of women;
Hermuntnr of the hard axe carved these –
I ought not to have spoken.
She stops abruptly and with a frozen
clearing of the throat, recommences

from the beginning, without expression
but faster, permitting no further
interruption. Later she lets me examine
briefly the rows of stick-figures,
leads me to daylight again.

Tonight we lie, you and I, darkness a dome
overhead. At least we are together,
our love a live thing, this room
not yet ransacked by whatever invader
will carve here, as on cold stone, his name.

Monflanquin

We follow the track to Monflanquin,
on either side the sheen of rippling grain,
past the graveyard with its flaked stone

and flowers preserved under bell-jars.
As we stand here a coach drawn by white horses
glides past. Is that the music of the spheres

and is it too part of a fantasy,
like the quivering pantiles, the sky
too blue to be real? Try though we may,

it is difficult in such an atmosphere
to realise we are no longer
the definitive selves we once were.

Such timelessness cannot last.
Before they go to waste
or become things of the past

on our return to more mundane
surroundings, the diurnal routine,
within us let us jealously retain

those moments by that honey-coloured château
where we stood arm in arm, as from an upper window
came soaring the overture to *The Marriage of Figaro*.

Fort Napoléon

(for Serge Baudot)

We sit entranced in the night air
watching a troupe of eight
actresses alternate as Alice,

the dew so heavy they slither
on the stage, till one goes barefoot
and the others follow suit. Finally

they vanish, leaving only the moon's
refractions – and a filigree
of drenched prints, where they had been.

Lot-et-Garonne

This the domain of fable, of ant and grasshopper,
invisible cicada and cackling jay. Facing
due east, the sunflowers shrivel. Over meadows
of maize, loop liquescent catherine-wheels.
Meanwhile in the arena between my feet
two crimson beetles, linked tail to tail,
tug one another across baked soil.

Surfeit of fruit; a season's abundance:
nectarine and peach in profusion; bruised
melon, going cheap. So we stroll, and buy.
Bergerac for today's trout, *vin de table*
for tomorrow's *ragoût*. Cheese too, *du pays*.
But keep being drawn to those fruit vendors,
bare arms steeped in wasp-teeming wares.

An hour's cycle-run through shaded groves,
the Château de Biron emerges dominant
on the skyline, visible for miles around.
Severe but for its chapels. Its most
renowned Seigneur beheaded by Henri IV:
now centuries later, bleached bone
in blood-drenched soil. The sky porcelain.

Below, Lacapelle-Biron bakes. Our bicycles
against a wall, we bring out water-bottles
to slake our thirst. Under cypresses, solitary
Protestants lie. The air resonates, like a bell.
A woman waters begonias; while across the square,
a sandstone dog grins – his haunches
so yellow, he could be carved from butter.

A dragonfly settles on my shoulder, a flicker
of azure. Even under lime and acacia,
the glare becomes scarcely tolerable. Last
night's thunder did not long clear the air.
So much, so soon to be distanced from.
Already in the orchard has begun
the steady thud-thud of ripe fruit falling.

Picture Framer

He takes a sliver of beaten gold,
specially prepared; extends it
on a knife-blade, steady handed
and scarcely daring to breathe,
over the frame he is working on;

then with a simultaneous
exhalation and practised
flick of the wrist, sends
it floating – to land face up
on precisely the right spot:

the gesture repeated,
with what seems
sublime indifference,
till the task is complete;
the frame lustrous, immaculate.

So is love, even after
a lifetime's experience,
at the mercy of flights
as hazardous as those
of gold leaf, through draughts of air.

The Boathouse

The boathouse is the worse for wear: cracked
pantiles let in rain; a shutter is unhinged, the pocked
weather-vane broken by some local sharp-shooter.
The landing-stage too has seen better days,
its boards rotting. Yet we visit whenever we can
this fading Estate, skirting the big house
and the love temple, with its beeches and planned
rhododendrons. One man has taken the place of eight
gamekeepers. Nor do minor royalty come as they did,
to bag the deer or hold their swinging parties.

Envisage the locals, deferential; the young
gentry, on holiday from boarding school
in the south, disporting themselves nightly.
See the ice-buckets bead, the champagne flow.
The wendy-house on the island, overgrown now,
must have seen many a Chekhovian scene,
or Bacchanalian, girls in flimsy dresses,
hair gossamer in the breeze; sheep's carcasses,
breeding maggots on which the brown trout fed,
straddled on wires across the water's surface.

Strange that our presence should overlay theirs
as we manoeuvre our clinker-built boat in pursuit
of stocked rainbows where, in early summer,
the mountain-ash extend their candelabra.
What will the future bring? Can one owner
with propriety retain such inherited *grandeur*?
Yet how transfer so inaccessible a property,
as some would decree, to the downtrodden?
No ready solution. Our own, who knows,
may come to be counted among 'those balmy days'.

Two Harrier jets wheel overhead; a reminder
of other priorities. Their roar lingers
long after they disappear. Time to row in.
The boathouse shimmers, in the aftermath of rain.
A mink, predator of a different order,
swims to the bank, a fish in its jaws.
In the subsequent near-silence,
intensified by our bow-ripple, I realise
we have not seen or heard the peregrine
this season: like ourselves, an endangered species.

Skye Poems

(for John and Bar Purser)

On arrival

Here for a break, to shake the mind free
from its dullness, I gaze out on a sea
alternately dazzling with troughs of light
and lost in mist. As I sit and write
you work away, literally overhead,

scraping your cottage's corrugations
with an old hoe, prior to applying tar.
Your implement grates and grates, so close
I feel I'm a turtle or some such creature
having its shell cleaned, barnacles forcibly

removed, with the detritus of the past.
Below, the Bay glistens fitfully.
Bright thoughts force an entry. Soon
the new man that I am must venture
outside, skull scoured, legs however unsteady.

Dawn, Drinan

I lie dozing in the early hours,
aware of some element missing.
Then it comes: a burst of hail
blattering on the corrugated iron
of the roof, like a blizzard
of rock-chips, before expending
itself on the shore at Kilmarie.

Dizzied, I recall the scramble
from Coir an Lochain to the ridge;
our straddling Sgurr Dubh na Da Bheinn,
a sheer drop beyond. The shower passes
as unexpectedly as it came.
Opening my eyes I see the room re-form,
the curtain opposite slowly redden.

Reminder

What remains of today's skyline
is enhanced or marred, according
to viewpoint, by this home-made chair.
Roofed over in Spartan fashion,
its circular peep-holes enable land
on one side, sea on the other,
to recur. Position it, climb in,
you have a sun-trap to boast of;
protection for inclement weather;
a bird-hide, for the eager visitor;
sentry-box even, its driftwood
thicker than any arrow-head. The one
concession to modernity – castors,
for mobility. Upended and fronted
it could prove an economic coffin,
were one to sit upright, not lie down.
Before leaving, I am to put it
in the peat-shed, for its proper safety.

Sabbath

Overnight the wind shifts
from south-west to north-east:
we are into a new season.
The Tourist Board seals
sunning themselves in Loch Slapin
have taken the money and run.

Those mountains that looked as if
you could lean out and touch them
have come clean: they were
contours in the imagination.
The blueness of the other side
might have been invented.

And it's the sabbath. Well, serve
it right – all week the Blackface
have been looking down their noses
like Wee Frees, at a spritely pigeon
with a birch-twig in its beak
masquerading as a dove of peace.

The islanders to the newly-weds

This gift is for you, its graded shades
of grey drawn one from each breed
of sheep on our Island – the wool undyed.

It will require to be teased and spun,
thereafter woven to whichever design
meets your fancy. Before then

there are the fitting means
of preparing the tweed. True romance
decrees the ritual of the dance:

place in a tub, cover with water;
then tread with vigour, the pair
of you, for not less than eight hours.

During the process, such activity
permitted as conforms with propriety.
We wish you happiness. And energy.

Bog myrtle

Evenly spread on bunk beds
in the room above, bog-myrtle lay
drying – till it was taken south

for beer-making. What lingers
is its scent – so that I imagine
some young couple trysting here

(not Diarmid and Grainne, but a less
fated pair), a blessing on them:
legacy of its fragrance, in the air.

Meanwhile I'll leave this poem between
the sheets. Will it curl curiously,
or just fade away? We'll see.

October Week

On my first day back I am drawn
towards Blaven. Despite driving rain
I park, put on Wellington boots
and set out. As I leave the track
and reach the tree-line, mists clear,
revealing an amber glare. Bog-myrtle,
crushed underfoot, releases its fragrance.
And I find my love for you, in absence,

grows more intense. If only, I feel,
by some miracle you could be here;
knowing even as I turn, spontaneously
eager, that it is a flight of fancy.
Except that, acknowledging where
I'd imagined you would be, over
Ben Meabost there rises one rainbow's
perfect arc, within the ghost of another.

*

I've realised I am spending the week
with an older man. He comes downstairs
a hairsbreadth behind me, and when I go climbing
imposes his limits. For him I pack a spare
pullover, leave the immersion heater on.

Could it be the green woolly hat I found
in a lay-by? Perhaps it was planted
by trolls. This morning while shaving
I was confronted by a puckered frown
peering from under it, grey wisps protruding.

He keeps telling me I'm putting on weight;
but I'm damned if I'll let him impose his diet.
If he has to rise during the night, that's
his problem. And when the time comes,
he can do his own clearing up.

*

We huddle as though in the lee of a dyke,
where there is none: myself, and those
admonitory selves who urged, 'Stay in,
you'll be drenched before you even reach
the stream, which in any case won't be passable.
And if you try to cross at the waterfall,
you'll find the face sheer glass.'

They were right, of course. 'Furthermore,
you'll have to cling to the buttress
lest a gust hurl you over.' Here
I last glimpsed a pair of eagles,
wheeling effortlessly over the scree,
past the impossible pinacle. I hug
the ground, anticipate a squall.

Instead, a lull: with it, that break
in the clouds I thought would never come;
and miles away, the flat summit of Raasay,
where obsequious Boswell danced his jig.

*

The elk-skull in the adjoining room
remains untouched by my presence.
He is lord of this place,

sustaining not merely visions
of pursuit over rough terrain,
torrents taken in their stride,

but the tremor of millennia
in the span of those antlers
before the hounds of Cúchulainn;

flanks that covered bogland
when Scotland and Ireland were one.
When I go, I leave all to him.

VI

Sights and Sounds

From my Cape Town hotel, an incessant
barking of dogs; in the Malay Quarter
the muezzin's interminable wail.
I twitch the curtain: a cockroach scuttles.
The preposterous sun splits Signal Hill.

Soon on the car radio, the mellifluous tones
of the English Service tell of the release
on Robben Island of an undisclosed number
of penguins; heavy news, in Afrikaans;
and on Springbok, 'the Rise and Shine Show,

setting you on your way, this Wednesday'.
Past the Hospital Bend intersection
where the accident rate, many years ago,
dropped temporarily with the installation
of a sign, 'Dr Barnard is waiting for you'.

Domains fragrant with thyme and rosemary;
then Groot Constantia, balm to the eye,
its facades exquisite as sugar-ice
against an azure sky. All porcelain
and honeyed furniture. Upstairs, a clutter

of Edwardiana: old 78s, gramophones
with the original horns. Tempting
to put them on, throw open the windows
and let loose a cacophony ranging from
'Now is the hour' to 'Excerpts from *Lohengrin*'.

On the Water

(for Gus and Nicky Ferguson)

An opportunity to observe close-up
those exotics I've been peering at
through binoculars, this past week:
the paradise fly-catcher, long tail
unmistakable; loerie with beaded eye;
most delicate, the lilac-breasted roller.
While I puzzle how to translate them
into print, a precocious bee-eater
settles on my pencil, as though
urging a place be found for him, too.

*

I stalk a crimson-breasted shrike,
willing him to come my way. Suddenly
in front of me he hops closer,
all neck-quirk, a blur in the lens:
I zoom in – missing him altogether.
A perfect opportunity muffed
through poor technique,
I go trawling the bird-book
for the finer points. But first
unfold my checklist, make another tick.

*

Beyond the inner circle of ibis and egret:
a decrepit stork who has lost all dignity.
Little more than a scrag of tatters
on a pole, he displays life's scars,
his once sleek jacket now a filthy misfit.
Pocked by puncture-marks, he is patently
an embarrassment. What they are saying to him,
conscience tells me, is 'Get out of it,
and take your cardboard box with you,
before you further lower the tone of the place.'

*

An irascible hornbill casts
a jaundiced eye, can't quite
credit it, so casts another.
Extends head and neck upwards
to emit vertical streamers
of sound. A second responds,
distance an irrelevance: like
Italian tenors, supposedly
addressing one another, but in reality
each playing to the back of the house.

*

Nesting marabou observe with an hauteur
ill becoming their role as scavengers,
seemingly unable to take in that they
and those others irradiating the air
are on the periphery of the action.
The jacana even, stilting dexterously
across the water-lilies, no more
than the *corps-de-ballet* for a purple
gallinule performing, faster than the eye
can take in, *entrechat* upon *entrechat*.

Interior

The tent resisting the night's chill,
I lie dreaming of giraffe and zebra,
kudu and princely sable. Above all
last night's elephant at the water-hole,
bearing the spirits of his ancestors.

Now the canvas panels glow: blue,
red and white – a cubed drapeau;
then to the howl of whirled
acacia, transporting the spirit,
as in a box-kite, high over Africa.

Pilanesberg

The thornveld is shielded from outside
by a raised lava rim; our camp, within
the stone circle of an Iron Age site.
Inside that, a ring of expended ash:
a dead trampoline – the world's navel.

Morning and night, all snake-fang.
But now an approaching whirlwind
sucks spirals of dust into the air.
No escape, should its crazy zigzag
turn our tamed beast to cavortings of fire.

Leopard

We stop with a jolt. Scarcely thirty feet away,
a dapple of light becomes a leopard in a fig tree;
hind-legs dangling, rosettes orange and russet.

So insouciant his descent. All muscular nonchalance,
he flows straight for us. Stops, and stares.
We absorb the amber of those wondrous eyes. Last

night's kill guzzled, he scrapes bloodstained grass.
Is gone. Such masterful grace. The stench of entrails
a merciful reminder we are observers, not participants.

Jedebe Camp

Trust

Spiky umbels of papyrus bob against my face
as Trust, the head poler, steers through
channels scarcely wide enough to take us.
Reaching an island of baobab, Trust places

a finger to his lips, points at a silhouette
bunched high on a fork: a Pels fishing owl.
I can just pick it out – a blotch of cinnamon
and white. Trust gives the thumbs-up.

Poling the mokoro back across the lagoon
he says he hopes his son will go to school
(as he didn't) and learn to read and write
(which his father did, in the diamond mine).

He names the water-birds in his own tongue
and Latin; showing no bitterness
at working, after deductions for food
and board, for a miserly daily rate.

Next day on the plane, I'll find myself seated
behind a lady who 'came all the way from Minnesota
just to see the Pels: worth every cent, believe me':
member of neither a rare nor an endangered species.

Water Two

Our boat moored to the reeds, Water Two
catches three tiger-fish, myself none.
Nor the elderly Zimbabwean in the bow.
Suddenly at 7 a.m., we are into a shoal

of barbel. After three revolutions
my reel screams, then slackens –
the leader bitten through. I land a bream.
The mozzies take over. 'Tiger next time!'

Alongside our catch, on the grass,
instead of the customary fly-box
the size 6 shoe of a former Miss S. Africa
here on a promotional tour. In the small hours

I think of her stretching those lissom limbs;
while in the next tent the Zimbabwean
laments Mugabe's latest sequestrations.
Hourly, the snuffle of hippo

in the surrounding swamp. Already, Okavango
a jewel, in the brain. After coffee and fruit,
I find my backpack speckled with birdshit.
The previous day's catch, fish-eagle bait.

Over the desert

Entering the Kalahari the pure waters
of the Delta, rather than form an estuary,
peter out in a depth of sand so great
even major earth tremors leave no trace

but are absorbed before reaching the surface.
Subjecting our lives, scarcely
more substantial, to varied analogy:
refreshment, or drought, of the spirit;

placing ourselves at others'
disposal; from this, to loss
of enlightenment over the centuries.
Below, a terrain *in extremis*,

dry valleys and fossil dunes
extending to the horizon and beyond;
the world's curve, billions of sandgrains.
Through a blur of condensation

imagine mirage-like, hazy and wavery,
an ancient Bushman and his wife, alone
in the thornveld, awaiting the hyenas
through whom they will join their ancestors.

VII

Ayrshire Coast

Sandy links and raised beaches...made Ayrshire a
prime resort for Victorian and later pleasure-seekers.
RIAS GUIDE: 'Ayrshire & Arran'

West Kilbride, Gailes, Barassie, Troon,
Prestwick, Bellisle and points between:
so the links courses of our schooldays
unfold like an apron of green baize
brooched by gorse and dune, down Ayrshire's
coastline. This year's Masters, watched
in comfort by satellite, contrasts
with that monochrome age, when first prize

in the *Daily Mail* Tournament (all of £250)
went to Dai Rees for 'four sturdy rounds';
his autograph, alongside Henry Cotton's neat
hand, a reminder of what we were desperate
to emulate – only to learn in life how rather
than the dream parabola adolescence yearns for
(golf's equivalent of the perfect iambic pentameter)
the ball dips and veers through unsupporting air.

Enforced holidays on Troon beach made the most
of ice-cream vans enveloped in sea-mist;
chittery-bites seized on; female underwear
seen surreptitiously, as one-piece swimsuits
were discarded – paleness of thigh and breast
projecting neither guilt nor embarrassment,
which in those days seemed not carnal, or remote,
but simultaneously peerless and innocent.

A different proposition when we danced
a decade later, to Harry Margolyes
and his Band, at Ayr's Italianate Pavilion
Ballroom; and on the prom on autumn
evenings, walking arm in arm, glimpsed
through fumbled skeins of blonde or auburn,
lighthouses blinking from afar; then
to return, our numb cheeks flecked with brine.

*

Despite erosion, the coastline scarcely
changed. Except, where we believed the breakers
would always surge purely, squalor has taken over;
successive tides jettisoning scum and debris.
You can drive on south toward Heads of Ayr,
gaze averted to Arran and its Sleeping Warrior.
But hard to stomach, the beaches where we sat
unfit for a European health certificate.

A history not short on brutalities:
where Alexander routed Haakon's invaders –
Nardini's wicker-chairs and brash *torchères*;
unmarked graves, and the occasional stone
where fleeing Covenanters were hacked down;
while in Dunure's black-vaulted dungeon
for the Commendator of Crossraguel's
basting, Cassilis 'spared not flaming oil'.

Confidently claimed Scotland's microcosm,
Arran preserves its own social schism:
the hotels in Brodick, Lamlash and Whiting Bay
part of a douce but rigid hierarchy;
coach-parties welcomed by some, not others;
guest-houses girt for the Glasgow Fair
when the crowds would mill, and glutted gulls
followed the churning of great paddle-wheels.

Even in this haven, shades of *timor mortis*:
of the glowing Academy girls we rowed,
one succumbing early to sclerosis;
others performing the offices, for the dead.
Amongst summer's specialties meanwhile
persists the democracy of the bicycle;
with rucksacked cohorts setting out to tackle
the rock-chimney of Glen Sannox, and Goat Fell.

*

The Season ending, B & B signs come down;
the daily ritual of the sheets ceases;
skimpy guest-towels are returned
to store. Arcades of fruit-machines
empty. Vacated caravan sites
reveal their own *mal du pays*.
More grave the varieties of silence,
year round, where diverse activities

once were: boat-building in harbours
made derelict; Ardeer's work-force
hit by the rigours of redundancy.
To freewheel down (or up) the Electric Brae
an ideal metaphor for the economy;
Culzean's castellations, provenance
of the rich; and on the skyline, defunct
Ailsa Craig, Cuchulain's curling-stone.

In a county of milk-yielding heifers,
creameries producing ersatz cheeses;
lace curtains still gracing Newmilns
and Darvel – but their heyday undone
by cheap labour from Japan. Pit closures,
dignity once attained at the coalface;
rails rusting from Doon to Dalmellington:
Cockburn's 'last place in Ayrshire where

with a good deal of primitive manufacture,
rural simplicity and contentment linger' –
its Age of Iron having come and gone...
Whisky aside, the one sacrosanct industry
centres on Alloway. Burns statues scan
a World which while paying lip-service,
reveals less and less his philosophy
of brotherhood, than Man's inhumanity to Man.

Map of Coningham

being the North Part of *Aire Shire*, by Thos. Kitchin (1718-84)

(for Gerry Cambridge)

This 18th century 'map of Coningham',
part-tinted, unobtrusively fits in
with our kitchen decor, its simplicity
in keeping with earlier watercolour days:
Kilmarnock central to its intimate universe,
as so it seemed; in identical type-face,
Craigy and *Eglintoun*; and like a wire
slicing cheese, one road aslant the Shire.

In my inner ear those years remain encased –
precise as birdsong, their crisp cadences.
Minimal brushstrokes meanwhile, under glass,
summon a parallel vision of the past:
a world of distinctive cattle, white and brown,
antique machinery, loads that are horse-drawn;
and industrious generations, who belong
to the soil as it, for a spell, belonged to them.

A rurality stoutly asserted, when at school
we resisted those determined to rinse
Scots from our mouths. Ours too a dual role,
would-be city slickers, lads about town
eager to flaunt, when following Killie,
the vocables of our industrial milieu;
till a visiting fan with fouler glottals
roared 'Get tore in at thae country yokels!'

Distance not simply framed fastidiously,
but scaled in accord with 'English miles';
degrees longitude, anachronistically
west not from Greenwich but from Edinburgh
whose inhabitants, wholly oblivious
of our lives' minutiae, would have been
shocked at the vehemence of our disdain
for the noses they supposedly looked down.

This later conceded as anti-snobbery,
itself supplementing a dichotomy
of urban and rural selves – identity
so split, as to feel an outsider either way;
remaining at heart uncertain if I stem
from town or country; born and bred a son
of the manse, yet experience most intense
in that half moon's cropped and tilled expanse:

few nightmares worse than a stallion
splintering stable doors, or hell more real
than the limepit into which a horse
and cart were sucked, when I was small.
So that despite gulfs of time and space,
a world remote but for a rectangle
on a wall, I still think of my shoes
holding a sprinkling of rich Ayrshire soil.

Spring

Ayrshire is breaking into leaf, you say,
then convey in detail sound and scenery,
fresh limes emerging, a grasshopper warbler's
whirring song. It makes me think of Daphne
fleeing Apollo, and her father's answer
to her prayer: leaves sprouting from her hair
and hands, bark shielding her quivering body.
The one a timely metaphor for the other:
the dew, escaping its lover's ardour,
leaving nothing but verdure, where
a moment earlier, it sparkled purely.
You'll be telling me next how lovers lie
languid under every laurel tree; Aurora
filling the air from Girvan to Dunure;
Arran's outline clear, across a wine-dark sea.

from **Early Days**

Connections

Changing trains at Glasgow Central *en route*
for a poetry workshop in Kilmarnock I visit
the bookstall which has, needless to say, none
of my volumes on display. Nor any sign
on the departures board of my connection,
I'm so early. Eventually it appears:
objective reality, at least, restored. Soon
the old litany: Dunlop, Stewarton, Kilmaurs...

As my fellow-travellers, secure in their
identities or otherwise, journey on
towards Sanquhar, Carlisle, my reception
counters expectation: a strummed guitar,
the car in a tarmacked space where rails once were,
set in cobbles, to ease the dray-horses' burden.
To an unaccustomed music, and hyacinths in bloom,
the decades dissolve, and we coast into town.

Mirror image

Evening drawing in, I revisit old
haunts: the Burns monument, smaller
than I recall; St Marnock's, trees squat
as ever; and facing the Dick Institute
the sandstone Academy, dominant on its hill.

Over a couple of pints in the Goldberry
I'm told I don't sound like I'm really
from Killie, the intervening years
having added an overlay. But things seem
to go smoothly. So that by the time

I reach the station I'm confident
I could pass for local. Till reflected
in the waiting-room window, I see
a familiar figure carrying a plastic
bag emblazoned *'Ayrshire and the Burns country'*.

Wild Flowers

I didn't know *lupinus polyphyllus* as such, in those days:
simply that our manse garden was rampant with displays
of varying blue; nor that this converging in colour
of massed spikes, year after year, was a reverting to nature.

Oblivious, we lay in their ribbed and scented dens,
bees blundering by, under clouds of chiffon. As intense
were the stained-glass windows we gazed at on Sundays,
the congregation dwindling – successive generations

heading for housing schemes, but still the appeals
for the fabric fund, the carillon of bells;
the burden ever greater, for fewer to bear.
Compare *epilobium angustifolium*, similarly

tall-stemmed, but a looser, fluffier flower,
its mauve spires pointed out by my mother
when we went for runs in the family car, till we'd cry
'Guess what, rosebay willow-herb!' Found mainly

on disused railways, it proliferates where factories were;
reminder of jobs lost, of bitterness and despair.
In abundance, willow-herb and lupin demonstrate
the slow dereliction of Church and State.

Terra Firma

The church of which my father was minister
lowered over my boyhood, its front elevation
imprinted on the retina; an endowed carillon
spendthrift expenditure of a sum more
practical if put towards the maintenance
of rotting roof timbers and friable sandstone.
Although latterly dwarfed by the Police Station
and Sheriff Court opposite, an architectural

survey recently lauded its structure
from hood-moulded main door to battlemented tower,
not to mention *the pulpit's fine expression*
of the crescendo of the Gothic revival...

We'd never have guessed (far less cared)
when as children we fidgeted on hard pews,
that those encompassing walls in future years
would be praised as *scholarly perpendicular –*
a paradox sharpened by the then snobbery
of the town's more class-conscious clergy
one of whom murmured, after his ordination,
'Of course St Marnock's isn't on the map, Conn.'
Throughout his calling, in ways I was then
too young to comprehend, he remained his own man:
voicing concern for single mothers, whom
the Kirk's committees saw as 'fallen women';

and believing an unfashionable ecumenicalism
the way to enlightenment, debating at Coodham
and courting the Kilmarnock Standard's abuse
by counting among his friends, RC priests.
As through a glass darkly, I have come
to a more comprehending admiration
for the industry and integrity
he must have channelled into his ministry –
rather than any inheriting of beliefs: partly
because he never exerted pressure
but permitted me to go my own way,
doubtless praying it would not be to purgatory.

Those moments uppermost, at a lifetime's remove,
of austere ritual, redeemed by love
under the lights of the Christmas tree;
and at harvest festivals, ripe sheaves
round the walls of the shadowy vestibule,
fruit heaped before the communion-table,
then the delivery of flowers and vegetables
by the Bible Class: a child's view of the tangible
manifestations of others' belief in Divinity,
not the tenets sustaining it. Today
the building stands, like a preserved dragon –
forbidding still, but no longer breathing flame.

Peace and Plenty

On autumn Saturdays we'd cycle
to Caprington Estate with its great
chestnut trees: the lawns littered,
each spiky bur split on impact,
ripeness preserved intact.

Pockets filled, we hurled up sticks
to dislodge what more we could –
eager to get at the Upper Crust
with their stately homes and shiny
Daimlers, the only way we knew.

Ingrained, a callow awareness
of revolutionary days, eggs thrown
at carriages, aristos done down.
Their ruined mansions seen later
as bombastic parodies of what they were;

our middle-classness an encumbrance
rather than aligning us
with miners' families
or those in the neat cottages
known as Peace and Plenty,

harking back to an age
presaging a New Dawn.
Hard to take, the fruits
of promise not justice
but a polarisation such

as we've seen; retributive
Government seeking scapegoats
among Society's weakest;
stooping to enlist folk-myth
in ways we never dreamt of.

Stolen Light

A shiver crosses Loch Stenness
as of thousands of daddy-long-legs
skittering on the surface.
In total stillness
thunderheads close in.

Lead-shot from a blunderbuss
the first flurries come.
The elements have their say;
the depths riven
as by some monster.

The impulse to run
hell-for-leather
lest this a prelude
to one of the Great Stones
clumping to the water.

A friend is writing
a book on poetry
and inspiration.
Brave man – imagine him
in flippers and wet-suit

poised on the edge:
a charging of nerve-ends
too rapid to track,
or underwater treasure
you hold your breath and dive for?

First Light

Near Nunnerie, where Daer and Potrail meet,
highstepping it through early morning mist:
a troupe of llamas; one brown, four white,
their head-erect posture midway between
goat and camel, last thing we dreamt we'd see.

Approaching the bank, they stop in unison
and stand motionless, maybe in contemplation
of their near perfect reflections, or simply
for a good nostrilful of us, then move on;
all but the largest, who gazes quizzically

as if asking, 'Do you suspect we exist
only as some mutation of the spirit
of the place? Have it as you please.'
Then dismissing philosophical fripperies
he turns and splashes through a hoop of light.

Return to Provence

Odd to find ourselves zigzagging
round fields of lavender as we did last time
seeking shelter from the rain.
See those swallow-tails, the air steeped in resin?

The harder we scour new horizons, the more
familiar the lie of the land. We slow down
not because the race is run, but for fear
we may catch up with who we once were.

Will we some day find the pines gone,
wells poisoned, no creatures near –
and wonder at what stage the change began?
Even if only in the imagination

light as pigeon-wings, by way
of a last gift, may our lips touch fleetingly.

Jawbone Walk

'It must have been all underwater
once. You're welcome to share my bench.
Where was I? Yes, a time when the entire

Meadows roared with the surge of seas.
Could you spare something towards lunch?
Thank you, sir. Yes, rather than trees

soughing, translucent waves rampaging. How else
do you imagine that arch got there? The ocean
has *haves* and *have-nots* too, you know, though

you might not think it. Never hear
of the scavenger crab? Don't suppose you
give it a thought. Must've been millions

of years before the Brontosauruses
came huffing this way, far less the Legions
who tramped north, only to disappear.

Much appreciated miss, no need to scurry away…
In the Pleistocene Age or thereabouts,
it must have been. Excuse me sir, have you the price

of a cup of tea? That's rich, I must say –
you wouldn't like to add a sandwich? Yes,
those jaw-bones have been around a long time.'

As he pockets my sub, and keen to remain
a one-off do-gooder, not form a habit,
I ask can we treat it as a season ticket.

Past bedraggled Sunday footballers,
kite-fliers and frisbee-throwers,
dogs single-mindedly at their business,

he heads down Middle Meadow Walk towards
the Infirmary outbuildings:
yellow-eyed, looming Mastodons.

Inheritance

When first we came to this city
there were nights we would lie
too tense to sleep for fear
the noises we could hear,
muffled blows, a woman's screams,
stemmed from real violence.
So it proved. In the small hours
she rang our bell, in her nightdress,
weals on her face, to use the phone.
One morning to our relief, they'd gone.
More pleasing sounds, if rarer silences,
now infiltrate our living space.

For all that, this a land ill at ease
with itself. Brutality decrees
its own choreography: small children
fastened at the wrist by coloured ribbon;
pavements laden with flowers
in cellophane. The fascination
of lens and screen forcing us
to choose, or not, to be voyeurs.
Short, from tempering justice
to compounding bestiality.
As deep, fear of being rendered,
through familiarity, immune to horror.

So are we at the mercy of the world we live in,
yet blessed as to some: one's son on heroin;
another traced to London, not heard of again.
The test, more and more, just to endure.
If so, what the likely adequacy
of our strain? Dawn comes. Reluctantly
I open the shutters, turn the radio on.
Scientists have found a link in human evolution:
a fossilised skeleton, adding to our ancestry
a further million years. What family-tree
can compete with primordial gloom, the cave-man
in you croaks sagely, to the cave-man in me.

Losing Touch

I *Losing touch*

I feel so confused. If only
I could sleep peacefully away.
We are living far too long nowadays.
Still, ninety is a good age, you agree?

Like a mantra, over and over,
between journeyings to far-off
resorts; exotic countries
and residences, vicariously

visited down the years;
now subterfuge experiences.
I envisage her fears
as so many furred moths

in a ferment between her
and the light; a journey
through a trance-like forest,
the abyss so close...

day-to-day life an instrument
she has all but forgotten
how to play – so long in a dusty
loft, its strings slack anyway.

II *Vantage point*

I seem hopelessly lost.
Worse than ever. I used
to be in a halfway house.
Nothing approaching this ...

Hardly a stone's throw
from the window, snow
powders Blackford Hill
where she played as a girl.

Little more merciless
than the ageing process:
ice filling the veins;
a hawk's glinting talons.

Her wrist frail on mine
I think despairingly of Man
and his Creator, exploding
from the Sistine ceiling;

yet when helplessly
she beseeches to be gone,
find I can pray only
that *her* will be done.

III *Oratorio*

She has shown no response
to Holy Week, as in earlier
days and down the years.
Nor do the signatures

on the Easter cards heaped
by her bedside convey other
than that they too relate
to an impenetrable past.

Bach at his most sublime
depicts Death, seen
through Satan vanquished
and Christ risen, as no more

than a gentle slumber
prior to entering Heaven.
The vision of her bowed
head, nodding slowly,

accentuates the mortality
invested in that fragile
frame. The chorus nears
its end. Jubilant voices soar.

Funerals

(for Don MacLennan)

You come across as Quixote
tilting at the Man with the Scythe
who hastening the natural
order, has frenziedly
done good friends down.

Your letters tell of orations,
shock of loss, and despair;
at last, consoling arms.
As for love, how answer
its whys and wherefores?

Today my steps lead me
through Warriston cemetery,
its unkempt headstones
nullifying any solace
poetry might offer.

Oh for a small son's innocence
who at such abundance
of skulls and crossbones,
asked why so many pirates
had settled in this place.

White-out

Blindingly from the east blizzards come.
The first flakes sizzle on the stove,
as the storm gathers momentum.
Were we in such a land, my love...

It is of you we think, children of Bosnia,
your ghosts like white birds passing
over, passing over: so that already
the sky is black with your wings.

Night Sky

Light hurtling at 186,000 miles
per second, what the eye sees
of that comet and its gas-trail
on its giddy jaunt through space
takes 12 minutes to reach us.

The power of lenses and mirrors
wondrous as ever. Even more
of a marvel, the way the brightness
in your eyes travels towards me
at the implausible speed of love.

Intricacies
(for Rupert)

Before he was any age, they'd set out
each morning for the rink at Richmond,
so that he could be on the ice by 6 a.m.

In subsequent years, he earned not only
the trophies adorning his room
but warmth of applause, a unique affection.

The ultimate barrier broken, things can never
be the same. From the heart's recesses
he goes flawlessly spinning, beneath boughs

bearing snow like blossom. Across
the limitless expanses of the imagination,
he pirouettes joyously – then is gone.

His skates' pure harmonies ring on and on.

Above the Storm

'At altitude, conditions will worsen.' Inevitably
the first snow comes at the top of the gully,
as I unzip my anorak and pour a mug of tea.
Sod's law; and Nature's too. As in real
life, things deteriorate when we least want it.

At this moment though, I'm assured your flight
will be above the storm (worst for 25 years
the weatherman said) as you head for Los Angeles,
then Auckland. I hope they're right, and that
your long-awaited trip gets off to a smooth start.

*

At some point during a storm-tossed night
I peer at the faintly luminous face
by my bed, try to calculate
where you might be. At eight-thirty
in the evening, you could well be out

for dinner with Angela and George:
a gathering too discreet to gorge
yourselves American-style, but capable
I'm sure of eating well. Sleep calls.
Bon appétit! I'll let you pay the bill.

*

Two midnights later. You will have flown
(if on schedule) over Hawaii, and soon
be crossing the International date-line:
short-cutting from yesterday to tomorrow.
As I stand at your plant-strewn kitchen window

my heart tells me there should be some sign
visible at least over your own tended garden.
No shooting-star – did I really expect one –
but in the gap between the tenements opposite,
the sky is decked with garlands of pure white.

*

Sunday. I wonder if you're worshipping
in the same neat church I sat in, when
so briefly there. Nothing Victorian,
but stripped pine, with modern carving.
A well-behaved New Plymouth congregation

sang rousingly, then gave the lengthy sermon
full attention – never wavering
(that I could see) as a line of ants came in
one window, skirted the organ screen
and on reaching the far wall, disappeared.

*

Since it is mellow afternoon with you,
treat this short section as a *billet doux*.
I picture you anchored in a bay of blue
where you enjoy, with John and Liffey,
a swim in water (why not the old cliché)

still crystal-clear. Laughter reaches me,
like tinkling bells. From the boat's side
come lappings of applause, as if on cue.
I send my love as, colourfully clad,
carefree you set, then light, your barbecue.

*

Your papyrus plant, which I was to water
on alternate days, forgotten utterly.
The extent of my neglect: its slender
stems are bowed; dried leaftips shrivel;
its elegant parasols, all forlorn.

For such mishaps, desperate remedies. I pour
bottlefuls in, night and morning. No sign
of recovery. Too late the familiar, bitter
lesson: little use a surfeit of affection,
once the initial damage has been done.

*

Your spirit meantime flits about the place,
from those items bought in auctions
in our early days, to the cushions
scattered in the sitting-room, the rummers
and yellow plates displayed downstairs;

elsewhere the angling of a lampshade,
consistent with where the pictures
look their best. And latest of all,
your newly-lined bedspread: untenanted
it keenly awaits you, discreetly autumnal.

*

And see, against the net curtains
like a screen print: the papyrus
in its brass bowl. Assiduously
cared for since my sin of omission,
it has recovered miraculously –

conjuring up visions of Nefertiti,
Thales proclaiming *water is all*;
the rushes Moses was left in,
by the Nile. Yet how convince
you I've hand-maidened it well?

*

What about: only yesterday I cut
its largest leaves into strips;
the pith beaten, and rolled
with mud substitute; then pressed
under the mattress on wooden slats

with fitting devotions, to produce
the flimsy parchment this is written on.
Forgive its clumsy hieroglyphs. Even
if you don't believe a word of them,
the important thing is: welcome home.

VIII

Ghosts at Cockcrow

Visitation

In pride of place on my work-surface
are an inkwell of weighted glass

and a black quill-pen, presented to me
when I left long-term employ;

a discarded life I heed less
and less, as the years pass.

But every so often with a hoarse *kraaa*
there squats on the sill a hoodie crow,

a gap in one wing where a primary
feather is missing. Teetering raggedly

it fixes me with a bloodshot eye
then flops, disgruntled, away.

Whether intent on repossessing
what belongs to it, or chastising

me for treating its lost quill
simply as a glossy symbol,

I recognise in it the beast
of conscience come home to roost.

The cat meantime sits by the fireplace,
content that nothing is amiss.

In the Garden

What is it about that bush, a golden choisya
my wife tells me, which catches the eye –

the abundance of leaves on display
in the sunrise, or the way

these range from lime green
to a lemon glow? This impression

of a nimbus induces some memory
I can't place. Then it hits me:

the Church hymnal
in the manse pew when I was small

bore the imprint of a burning bush, over
the inscription *nec tamen consumebatur.*

This version comes untrammelled
by such baggage. A thrush with speckled

breast struts unecclesiastically
beside it. And that butterfly

I see as more likely to be Li Po
dreaming, than the alter ego

of a Presbyterian divine
sermonising on sin.

Ministrations

The ghosts who haunt us
are not those who belong
to our superstitious past

or to childhood fancy,
gliding unconcernedly
through solid walls, clanking

chains in dank corridors
or descending stairways,
their heads in their arms.

Equally white-vestured
they are the apparitions
who will rise ahead of us

bearing pills and bedpans,
holding our hands
in unfamiliar rooms;

in gauze masks attending
during the operation,
helping to alleviate pain;

then when the day comes
drawing the sheet finally
over our flaccid faces.

Upon which it is we
who will dissolve, not they.
Best believe in them.

Heirloom

Learning on moving house to Edinburgh
that my grandfather's licensed grocer's
had been in the High Street
made me feel less an interloper,
than one who has been long away.

Next door to the police station
he would leave out, on wintry nights,
a dram for the man on the beat.
And his special-constable's baton
bearing the city's coat of arms,

presented during World War One,
hung in our front porch for years
on its frayed leather strap, for decoration
but within easy reach in the event of intruders.
Only to end up lost, presumed stolen.

Growing Up

On Sundays I would take the boys to play
in Holyrood Park (we once had to knock
on the Palace door and ask for our ball back).
At that age the competitive spirit was high:

they'd fly into the tackle hell-for-leather
till I'd warn, 'Any more fouls of that kind,
we're off home', then have to stick to my guns
or lose face (*hoist* and *petard* come to mind).

Was this instilling a sense of fair play,
or simple abuse of power? I remember
the small group trudging back to the car,
the sullen silence throughout the journey.

Six-footers now, they're able to cope
with life's greater buffetings, take mature
decisions affecting themselves and others.
But I wonder, did their father ever grow up?

City Interlude

Rain stotts on the setts and bounces
from David Hume's bull-brows.
Outside the main entrance to St Giles

a young woman in a white dress
is lifted carefully from a wheelchair
and placed in the lap of a kilted piper

to have her photo taken. Their faces
seek the light. Then, the dress almost
transparent, she crooks an arm round

her male companion, who carries her
to a taxi that has been ticking over.
It drives off, raising a cloud of spray.

All this watched impassively by a pair
of wardens who now return to the fray.
The piper pumps his bag and starts to play.

Autumn Walk

Strolling through the Meadows
a few days after my birthday
I make the discovery
that advancing age has invested me
with a cloak of invisibility.
Close behind are two students. One,
her coat swinging open, displays
a bejewelled belly-button,
the other has hair like a pony's mane.
'I tell you, I waited and waited...
even turned over, lay on the bed
on my back. I can't make head
nor tail of him, after all the come-on.
How about you?' 'No problem,
the difficulty is stopping him
before I'm worn out. Have to find
you someone for the weekend.'
They head for the David Hume Tower,
their breath like plumes in the chill air.
I walk on, pondering growing old.
The leaves turn to russet and to gold.

Edinburgh Thaw

The snow sullied as quickly as it came,
already yesterday is like a frame

from a forgotten film. Closest to home
the flowering cherry in our garden,

no longer burdened by the weight
it bore, again flaunts its own white.

At street intersections, Christmassy figures
revert to being *Big Issue* sellers.

Uncannily, slush shifting on the bronze rider
in St Andrew Square makes him appear

to move – like Mozart's Commendatore;
while in the courtyard of the Assembly

Hall a pigeon, like a dove of peace, lands slyly
on Knox's upraised arm, and meets his eye.

Close Names

(for James Robertson)

Fishmarket Close and Fleshmarket Close,
preserved down the centuries, still
strike a chord; like Old Tolbooth Wynd
and the long gone Luckenbooth stalls,
their silver hearts intertwined; while
Hammerman's Entry summons
the bellows' roar, ring of iron on iron;
and Dunbar's Close, Cromwell's
Ironsides billeted after battle.

Sugarhouse Close and Bakehouse Close
boast their own past and function –
not quite Dippermouth and Porterhouse,
conjuring up images of New Orleans
cutting contests and tailgate trombones,
but suggestive of a distinctive music
resounding in the Royal Mile
throughout Scotland's history,
theirs a ground bass of a different kind;

now jaunty, the banners streaming,
now plucking the heartstrings
like the Blues, in the realisation
of things lost, the end of an auld sang.
As with the Blues too, a lingering
undertow of loss and deprivation:
the start of a new age – yet the city's
division into haves and have-nots
never more discordant than today.

Cappella Nova at Greyfriars' Kirk

Rare as whorls of gold-leaf floating in air
the cadences of Carver and the Inchcolm
Antiphoner are followed by the radiance
of a present-day elegy for Colum Cille –
he should have been Scotland's patron saint.

Emerging afterwards into a grainy twilight
(itself enough to make you catch your breath)
and walking past the domed tomb of bluidy
Mackenzie to where the Covenant was signed
it fully registers that the priestly composer

of another piece, all exultant counterpoint,
was Robert Johnston who fled to England,
charged with heresy, after the martyrdom
of Patrick Hamilton by Archbishop Beaton:
a torch which ignited the Reformation.

How swiftly beauty and horror intertwine,
the one so often a means of purging
the other; in this instance the singers
our intermediaries, the dark abyss bridged
by such poise…such perfect harmonies.

Footage of RLS

Fade in. Opening credits over wreathings of haar;
then South Seas blue. Long shot of early removal
from Howard Place, though still within reach of the effluent
Water of Leith. Cut to the grandeur of Heriot Row.
Later in flashback, the fevers and forebodings
which presaged so much of his writing; that hacking
cough banishing him to the Land of Counterpane.
Subliminally in the background, Blind Pew tapping.

Aerial shot of the Pentlands. Dissolve to the Cévennes
where under starry skies he declares his desire
for the woman he would marry. Clips of their Silverado days,
his 'mountains of the moon', the icy cage of Davos.
Superimposed on cascading pieces of eight, a ghostly
hand writing to satisfy his daemons and foot the bills
for the hangers-on with their fancy tastes, that wastrel
Lloyd. Drifting in and out of shot, his 'dusky tiger-lily'.

Jekyll and Hyde are playing in an adjoining auditorium
(on split screen of course). Rushes of Weir of Hermiston
litter the cutting-room floor. The life he is enacting
smacks increasingly of a fiction. The publicity stills
no longer have him coughing up blood (bad for business)
but gazing enigmatically out of frame, except for one
where he soulfully eyes the lens. By the third reel
he seems to be yearning not for Belle (the B movie)

but for Allermuir and Caerketton, places he knew
he'd never see again, his Edinburgh long gone, so many
poems and stories written for the shadow of the child
he had been, part of a magic-lantern show; the dandy
and buccaneer in him exhausted. For the final scene
a double must have taken over: those grieving Samoans
hacking through jungle to lay him to rest on Mount Vaea.
The lights come up. He sits smiling at the back of the cinema.

Writer's Block

Various ploys advocated to keep at bay
this beast they say can induce frenzy.
Some try 'hot writing' – like swimming
underwater… not coming up for air.

For stimulation one troubled troubadour
set his loved-one naked on a divan. Keats
put on his best shirt and shoes. Wordsworth
bemoaned its *long continued frost*. It made

Conrad want to howl and foam at the mouth.
Samuel Johnson didn't beat about the bush:
A man may write at any time, if only he will
set himself doggedly to it. Nearer our day

Gore Vidal takes the biscuit: *Something*
I've never experienced. First coffee.
Then a bowel movement. Then
the muse joins me. What more to say?

Ghosts at Cockcrow

Once, on this earth, once, on this familiar spot of ground, walked other men and women, as actual as we are today, thinking their own thoughts, swayed by their own passions, but now all gone, one generation vanishing after another, gone as utterly as we ourselves shall shortly be gone like ghosts at cockcrow.

G.M. TREVELYAN,
An Autobiography and Other Essays

Appearances

As the train draws out, the man seated
in front of us meticulously places
his jacket on the rack, opens his briefcase
and settles to a sheaf of papers, oblivious
of the mobile phone opposite, its owner
signing off loudly: '*bisous, mon cœur*'.

Designer glasses gleaming, body
language assured, he could be an *avocat*,
a partner in an art gallery, even a *député*
commuting from Paris to his constituency.
Though something trim and lithe belies
the customary trappings of the good life.

Then I notice he is poring over exam papers
on 'English comprehension', neat hieroglyphs
filling every available space in the margin
before he totes up the underlinings, gives
a mark, shuffles the pages and moves on.
He keeps at it, schoolmasterly, head down.

On our first morning in Dijon, the Hôtel Buffon
offers a pleasing precedent: how of the Comte –
in Drouais' portrait trig in embroidered waistcoat
and powdered wig, and looking for all the world
the *grand seigneur* – David Hume said 'he looks more
like a marshal of France than a man of letters'.

Notre-Dame, Dijon

The Cathedral's capitals look down
unperturbed, their carved features
interchangeable with today's
albeit more eroded, eyes less focused
than our own on the diurnal routine.
Outside, remnants of smashed stone
reiterate what these blind eyes
might have seen: not in this instance
destroyed like so many, during
the Revolution, but subject to a fate
as wanton as it was arbitrary:
a gargoyle, falling from high
on the main tower, flattening
a passing money-lender. This,
in a city like most others teeming
with usurers, a bad move. With little
love for the Christian society by whom
they felt excluded, the remainder
got together and using their hated
powers, had the rest hacked down.

*

In the wake of visiting cathedral after cathedral,
absorbing the glory of tympanum upon tympanum,
the depthless blues and rich reds of rose-windows,
two images cling from the *église* Notre-Dame: one,
of the wooden Virgin (claimed the oldest in France)
so badly damaged at the time of the Revolution –
arms and legs hacked off, the Christ child gone –
she is draped in a white sheet (and wearing a crown
of glistening gold); and as we leave by the great
west front, of a drenched mendicant in green
who, sensing our approach, lifts the heavy latch
and holds open the oak door for us to exit –
then with a twirling half-bow, accepts the small
change he is given, with a smile not quite right.

Musée des Beaux Arts

A row of terracotta figures
on fluted pedestals convey
an astonishing immediacy
of head-tilt and expression,
their setting and wig-styles
the only visual giveaway
that they are not of today.
That...and arguably
a dominance of eyeline,
an aura of hauteur, over
the assembled hoi-polloi.

*

Above the tombs of the Dukes of Burgundy
in the *Salle des Gardes* hangs a tapestry
depicting the raising of a siege by the Swiss,
the square tower at its centre visible today
from the windows of an adjoining room.

But what catches the eye is the vast effigy
of Philippe the Bold and his consort, supported
on all sides by a stooped procession of mourners,
cowled heads drooping over marble lineaments,
mortality rendered in all its implacability.

For such a memorial to be ready on time,
its decorative carving necessarily begun
many years before the Duke was finally taken.
A double burden: theirs an unknown deadline;
for him, a race it would be no joy to win.

Vézelay

Our taxi-driver forgetting to come and collect us
for the ten-kilometre return journey to the nearest
station, our dismay at the thought of having to apply
luggage-less to some *chambre d'hôte* was wholly

at odds with the earlier discovery
that in the days when this had been a stopover
for penitents and pilgrims on the road to Compostela
hundreds slept rough, each yard of the street for hire.

Hotels

In each one, we are no more tangible
to the other residents than they to us:
muffled closing of doors, disjointed chatter,
hasty release of water in the small hours;
at dawn a clatter of keys, crunch on gravel.

*

At 2 a.m. I look out. The window directly
across the courtyard is unlit. Then
by an invisible hand, in the half-dark,
its net curtain is drawn slowly back.

*

Here each room has, instead of a number,
the name of one of Napoleon's Maréchaux –
twenty-six in all, their grave features
reproduced on a set of key-medallions
and postcards purchasable from reception.

When asked if their military ghosts roam
the corridors, the *patronne*'s look hardens.
But early next morning, no window open,
our swagged curtains seem to billow in,
their tops resembling ruffs, the heads gone.

In Transit

Returning from Auxerre we meet
other expresses, every seat empty
or passing at such speed, their passengers
are rendered transparent: either way
ghost trains, crossing fertile Burgundy.

ROULL OF CORSTORPHIN

He has taen Roull of Aberdene,
And gentill Roull of Corstorphin,
Two better fallowis did no man see
Timor mortis conturbat me.

WILLIAM DUNBAR,
'Lament for the Makars'

There is a poem in the Bannatyne Ms called Rowll's cursing...
Lindesay also mentions ROWLL; but there is no distinguishing
between the two poets of that name.

Sibbald's Chronicle of Scottish Poetry, Edinburgh 1802

Brissit* brawnis and broken banis,   burst
Strife, discord and waistit wanis,*   homes
Crookit in eild,* syne halt withal –   age
These are the bewteis of the fute-ball.

ANON,
'The Bewteis of the Fute Ball'

1 Roull Posited

Whilst out hunting King David, separated
from his attendants, was heavily thrown
and about to be gored by a hart *with auful*
and braid tyndis – whereupon, a cross
placed miraculously in his hands, the beast
fled. He endowed an Abbey on the spot
with the *holy rood*; later, on a narrow
isthmus, founded the chapel of CORSTORPHIN.

A *sair sanct for the crown* maybe, and more
Norman than Scot, but for all that 'father
of the fatherless... best of all his kind'.
From then on the monks fed the poor;
where three centuries later Adam Forrester,
twice provost of EDINBURGH, would lie
in effigy, arms crossed, his armorial
bearings three buffaloes' horns stringed.

Could Roull have taken holy orders here,
catching carp or brewing ale for the brothers;
penning verse from matins to compline,
at the last, to drown in the brimming lea?
Or did *'gentill'* denote a patient dominie
instilling through Wyntoun's *Chronicles*
pride of nationhood, a concept of chivalry
in many later to be slain in battle?

No way of telling if he was a plague victim
or survived to old age; extolled his
mistress in royal-rhyme stanzas or caught
nature in cantering couplets. Yet that one
naming by Dunbar enough to make him –
allowing for the trudge from the Castle,
the cleansing Water of Leith between –
the capital's earliest recorded poet.

2 At Court

What a flyting in the Great Hall: Dunbar
kicked off, then Kennedy took the bait.
First one declaimed, the bit between his teeth,
then the other, even gustier than before,
each raucously varying his angle of attack:
it was as if the ground under our feet shook.

In masterly metre, Dunbar dazzlingly derided
Kennedy's cack-handedness, in surely one
of the most sustained swathes of mockery
and contumely ever, so cutting you'd expect
his victim to run off whimpering, tail between
his legs. Not a bit of it: back comes Kennedy,

switching tack, comparing his fine lineage
to his antagonist's (not without blemish),
and defending his renegade *Heiland tongue*
against Inglis. In retaliation, a fireworks
display so coruscating as to seem diabolic,
setting off a cacophony of shrieks and guffaws.

Just as they seem about to come to blows
(mere fisticuffs, after this, an anticlimax)
his Majesty steps forward, declares honours
even. Perspiring, Dunbar grins. Kennedy
lifts a leg and unleashes a prolonged fart
which is instantly declared *hors concours.*

Meanwhile Roull, of a gentler school
and ill at ease with such crudities,
side-stepping the toadying courtiers
slips out and heads back to Corstorphin,
where in the shade of a seeding sycamore
he will sit penning his tender love poetry.

3 To His Cousin in Aberdene

I retain mellow memories of your visit
and of learning much from you, anent
metre and rhyme. And seeing as I do
poetry's prime purpose as the interplay
of nature and the affections, trust in return
you will elevate your subject-matter:
I'd hate future exchanges between us
to degenerate into flytings, even in fun.

As to health, I hope neither of us will require
the visitor whose repertoire takes in the severing
of limbs and opening of the body's cavities:
diet of sweet herbs rather, to ease our ageing.
That is to say, despite rubbing shoulders
with Physics and Barber-Surgeons, I aim
not to let them practise on me – but quietly
to pursue my chronicling of the seasons.

And in an indeterminate age (heather-clumps lit
to keep my house decontaminate) give thanks
for a loving wife's contours, sons grown
to manhood; content here at Corstorphin. From
a nearby doocot, a constant whoo-whoo-ing.
As for immortality: the Makars' flowering
ensures our generation will never be forgotten,.
timor mortis non *conturbat me*...

4 His Cousin's Reply

Delighted to hear there is life
in the old dog yet, your wife
a sweet haven for your
desires. Have no fears
regarding my verse: the great
Dunbar I too prefer when aureate.
But high on my list, such scoundrels
as steal my capons and fat fowls:

*Cursit and wareit be their werd**   fate
quhyll they be levand on this erd;
hunger, sturt, and tribulation,*   strife
and never to be without vexation...
povertie, pestilence or poplexy
I wish them, dum deif as edropsy,
the cruke, the cramp, the colica,*   lameness
the dry boak, &c. &c...

My stay vivid in the mind's eye,
several new poems at half-cock
describing the Castle on its Rock.
But I grew leery at the notion
of a royal tooth extraction.
Nor could I settle in Corstorphin:
after Aberdeen I need the sea –
its smash and sigh soothing to me.

But now I am home again
what hurts is the derision
of those who cry 'Butter fingers'
at my pig's bladder blunders.
How convey what hackers
they were who routed us?
But let them venture north,
by God we'll stuff them.

5 Roull on Musik Fyne

Nothing to the foul play of the choristers
at the Abbey of Scone. The worst,
sprightly loons who till we tackled them,
headed down each wing like a battalion
of demented gulls, cutting in on goal.
By the end, we were thrashed twelve-nil:
agile tenors in midfield, their last line
a bass-baritone built like a Scots pine.
All in all, despite our supporters' curses,
we had to admit they'd tanned our arses.

Later though, the radiance of their singing
in the Chapel Royal touched the heartstrings;
the Augustinian canon Carver, sturdy
enough to pass as *L'Homme Armé*
(and usurp the tune) transfiguring them
with his interweaving harmonies...
Lure them to Aberdeen, if they'll consent
to fight their way over the Cairn o' Mount
with its snow-swirls and snell nor-easters,
carrying their harps, lutes and tambours.

Is not our progress through life
a search for harmony, amidst darkness;
a blank parchment, awaiting the hand
to make of us an illuminated manuscript,
disponing both beauty and durability?
The King? He offers Carver commissions,
confident each motet will bring such balm
to his spirit as may help him forget
the burden of the iron chain he wears
as penance for his father's murder.

6 Insomnia

You say you can't sleep? By the doocot is the place:
under the eaves, the constant burbling of ring-doves;
and this the season for bees in the overhanging limes,
their lulling register between oboe and viola d'amore.

If that has no effect, try listing alphabetically
your favourite Saints: Adelaide and Aidan for starters.
The rocking of a moored boat soon induces slumber –
but not for sleep-walkers or the nightmare-prone.

With luck, a guttering candle will do the trick. Failing
which I wish you a clear conscience, the slumber
of the innocent. If that's too dull, the balmy haven
arrived at through impassioned hours of love-making.

7 Plaint

Under construction at Newhaven, to inspire terror
in any would-be invader, the *Great St Michael*
a triumph of the shipbuilder's art, two hundred
and forty feet long, bulwarks proof against shot –
and superintended by his Highness in person.

For this, every wood in Fife but Falkland
laid waste. And two hundred oak trees felled
for the hammer-beam ceiling in Stirling's
great hall. Lost for lifetimes to come. A marvel,
if one day we will have any forests at all.

8 Time of Plague

If I die first of us two, I'd rather
quietness than any ritual rend the air.

Nor any casting of ashes: on some high
hill we climbed, simply say goodbye.

And if beloved you be first taken
I'll do, however weakly, what I can

to treasure the living you. I'll try
in other words, to mourn with dignity.

But should either of these boys,
through mischance, predecease us

I'll hack out the God of Stone
and confront him with it – till one

of us lies broken, bone from bone.

9 To His Wife

The richest gift age can confer
is our growing old together,
not apart from one another.

But even more of a wonder:
loving you for what you are –
not just for what you were.

10 In Seiknes

If ever you do leave me, luve,
    'twill be a day o' dool.
The day that I leave thee, my luve,
    is the day I lie i' the mool.

For tho to leave this life we're laith
    I fear that day will daw
when in despite o' oor mortal aith
    the ghaistly cock sall craw...

11 Roull on Death

In the midst of *Life*, saith
the preacher, lurks *Death*:
yet still those who try
to bring it on more speedily.
Witness the Italian abbot
with whom James is presently
in thrall (among his promises,
to make gold from base metal)
who leapt from the wall
of Stirling Castle, only to fall
and smash his thigh-bone: his
excuse, that among the feathers
forming his wings were hen
quills which coveted the earth,
not the skies. All to counterfeit
King Bladud of old, who set
out decked similarly but took
a more grievous tumble, to
land on a temple of Apollo –
thereby breaking his neck.
No need to seek Death out:
the venerated Daubigny
on a visit to this country
sat at the King's right hand
at a tourney in his honour,

then collapsed in all his finery
while sampling our wine-cellars;
his blood, like best Burgundy,
a rampant tide. What a bustle
of ambassadors and courtiers.
His singular benefaction,
putting for a week Corstorphin
at the centre of the Universe.

12 Ghost of Roull

No poem of mine extant: would this were due simply
to time's vagaries, Gutenberg's revolutionary invention
supplanting the makar's flowery hand – if earlier,
I might have survived in manuscript form; later
through Chepman and Myller, preservation in print.

Even then such a debt to Bannatyne, not least
for Henryson's Fables – else unattributable,
those jewels in Scotland's crown; in their midst,
my cousin cursing whoever brak his yard and took
his hens: *blak be their hour, blak be their pairt.*

I still have his letters, stanza after stanza
on the reverse, blurred by candle-wax;
a fall putting paid to his seagoing and scavenging.
As for myself (ample scope to ponder since)
more likely lack of merit than Fate denied me

a drooling posterity, even as 'Anon'. At least
our presence in Dunbar's drum-roll of a Lament
(he outlived me little more than a year) confirms
our transient existence and that of our verse,
the whilk (for a spell at least) made readers rejoice.

Pursuing the *lilt of dule and wae*, hard how James,
having set himself up as a Renaissance
Prince, should have taken so many with him
at Flodden: one of Scotland's worst own-goals,
from a refusal to listen to the voice of reason.

Recorded that the Scots and English first tilted
at fute-ball at Bewcastle, Cumberland, in 1599:
one man disembowelled, but seemingly
sewn up again. Four years later, the Union
of the Crowns, a Golden Age bewilderingly

undone. Since then, rule by sword or pen;
pendulum swing of peace and war, amidst
the world's fears and turbulence. At home
the test, to this day, whether Scotland retains
the will to grasp the thistle, not the thistledown.

POST SCRIPTUM

The Barber-Surgeons to King James IV

We the Barber-Surgeons of Edinburgh, gratified at the granting
of the Council's Seal of Cause, applaud your Majestie's probings
into the workings of the body, its ailments and cures. Neither
blood-letting, nor amputation and excision, lightly undertaken.
Yet the climate one of suspicion, witness Robert Henryson's
'*Sum Practysis of Medecyne*', scurrilously deriding *lechecraft*
and *feisik* alike – and by insinuation ourselves. Were we to wield
our instruments as he does his quill, the cleansing Water of Leith
would soon be the River Lethe. That said, as much quackery
in his calling as among our fellows: how many makars
worth their salt – most seeking truth through verse as likely
to find it up their erse. Mercifully not all tarred, with the one
brush...Were we the fraudulent cuckoo-spits he suggests,
we might belabour him with reciprocal curses. Suffice
to say his legal brethren in Dunfermline can keep him.
On another tack, Majestie, a modest plea. Pledged to honour
our calling in time of strife and plague, we are sore put upon
mending cracked skulls and broken shins from the fiery
pursuit of fute-ball. If not banned (or the worst hackers
booted out) could we humbly petition for a royal decree
preserving Holyrood Park for the more seemly sport of archery?

In the Museum of Scotland

I come across a white horse in a glass case,
decked with period artefacts each in its place:
saddle studs and plates, silvered harness junctions,
slivers of body-armour, and from muzzle to ear
ornate fragments of chamfron – not as a work of art
but displaying each item's ancient function.
Going to bed that night, I cannot but wonder
what of your "you-ness" might be deduced
from the strewn scarves, the array of bracelets
on the dressing-table, the jet and greenstone beads;
and what of custom and appearance, in those items
spilling from your wardrobe, could be implanted
in the mind of someone who did not know you.
My good fortune lies in having no need
of such accoutrements to conjure up
the warmth and gracefulness they enhance,
the living likeness of their milk-white steed.

Eclipse

The city spills light. But the moon,
in a clear sky, holds its own,
diaphanous and vulnerable,
a sliver of rime – till
full circle again,
the eclipse might never have been.
Tempting when all returns to normal
to forget what made us marvel,
or wonder if it really happened.
Back in bed, I slip a hand
gently across, touch your shoulder,
just to make sure you are still there.

My Lady

Increasingly I come to think of you not as my Madonna
of the Mountains, though that too in happy times, the air
crystal round you; nor my Lady of the Azaleas, Flora
of our city-centre sit-ootery though you undoubtedly are;

not primarily my Confidante of the Opera; nor despite
those heaped-up tomes, Queen of Quattrocento Art
and Sculpture. But at moments like this, my study right
over your kitchen, Diva of the Wonderful Smells. Saliva

glands drooling, I picture you amidst spice-canisters,
adding herbs to steaming casseroles, stirring in mystery
ingredients, reciting potions over bubbling tureens,
your cookbooks well-thumbed and worshipful as holy

writ. I imagine you moving so aromatically
from one cornucopia of culinary delights to another
that rather than concentrate as I ought on poetry
I end up pondering which wine is most likely

to enhance what we'll be eating, hoping you will permit
this indulgence, as a mode of saying *bon appétit*.
Afterwards my errant memory rightly earns the riposte:
'Why not add My Lady of the Binbag to the list?'

On the Summit

Having scaled Ben Vorlich and Stuc a' Chroin,
from above mist-level suddenly it was like seeing
Scotland unveiling: Ben More and Stob Binnein;

further west, the whaleback and scythe-like arête
of Ben Nevis. The joy of each summit,
its mastery a defiance of limits.

Not just Munro-baggers – many a Corbett
as tricky, no clear route marked out –
our unstated aim is to resist the onset

of age, or give that impression while
we can, aching limbs part and parcel
of a process testingly physical

at the time, then once home again,
triumphant in its reconstruction
after a hot bath, over a gin and lemon.

Best relive each moment for all it's worth,
before those photos of out of breath
gnomes in anoraks bring us back down to earth.

Piazza del Campidoglio

In the thirty years since I visited Rome solo
I'd looked forward to returning with you
and to your first glimpse of the Campidoglio,

by far the loveliest square I've ever seen.
For weeks prior to our going, I'd imagine
you climbing the steps then pausing to take in

Michelangelo's design, flanked by the Capitoline
Museums; smack in the centre the great bronze
of Marcus Aurelius on horseback, gazing down.

Only it turned out differently. Climbing
from the Forum meant our approaching
from the rear – somehow so disorienting,

such a marring of anticipated perfection,
as to be the shuddering of a fault-line. When
eventually I took your hand, something had gone

and I'd tarnished what I wished you
most to treasure, that first miraculous view
of a beauty which, momentarily, embraced you.

Once we were inside, mercifully
the wonder of the artworks on display
took hold – Cupid and Psyche's butterfly

kiss almost within reach of the Dying Gaul,
then the other rooms and corridors until
we were overcome by the glory of it all.

Can there be moments too precious to bear,
or an irrational undercurrent of fear
at having to preserve, for the remainder

of our days the convergence of a particular
time and place, like not spilling water
brimming in a vase, however

steep the path? Either way I love and admire
you, for your wonderment, all the more –
although I suppose there will linger

a disquietude that were we to arrive together
at heaven's portal (Elysium, if you prefer)
I'd most likely spoil that too, out of terror.

The Actor's Farewell

It faded on the crowing of the cock.
Hamlet, I. i

Even in my heyday, I never played the Prince:
Horatio in rep, Laertes at school performances,
but never Hamlet in his black doublet and hose.
In contrast I remember the frisson of first striding
the battlements, in the glinting armour of the Ghost.

For a spell my speciality was not just doubling
but despite being stabbed behind the arras,
trebling as Polonius and First Gravedigger.
But that meant reappearing at the final curtain:
my preference, simply to vanish into darkness.

Even then I felt compelled to await heaven's
remonstrance; Hamlet mesmerised in his hall
of mirrors, driven to the rim of madness;
or from the safety of the wings, to watch Claudius
and his heartless queen get their comeuppance.

Whilst these and the others were drawn
from Holinshed or Thomas Kyd's tragedy,
the Ghost was purely Shakespeare's invention.
Each night I went on I sensed hovering round me
all those who had played the role previously.

Sometimes on tour things would go wrong:
once a rostrum not properly set, on my exit
I stepped into thin air; or some half-pissed idiot
missing his cue, a late *cock-a-doodle-doo* and thud
screwing up *'the morn in russet mantle clad'*.

But the great fear (ask any actor), my memory
going. Till a bright SM recorded my speeches
for me to mime to. Then one matinee the machine
went haywire; my jaws opening and closing
like a demented goldfish, to a frenzied whirring.

The derision of the gods, the last straw. That
and a director who reduced the Ghost's
presence to a trick of the light. Time to call it
a day. By then I was having second thoughts
anyway: didn't I trigger off the whole action...?

Mind you I learned not to overidentify
with my role (in my view Stanislavsky
could addle the brain); and despite
the skeptics, clung to the assurance
that Shakespeare himself believed in me.

The one lingering frustration
about which nothing could be done
was how in production after production,
despite resolution of the revenge theme,
Old Hamlet's soul remained unshriven.

As for the new minimalism, increasingly
I recall those gloriously costumed runs:
irrevocably gone, yet in spirit they remain.
The ultimate cockcrow? I'll be ready when
the time comes: '*Adieu, adieu! remember me.*'

Angel with Lute

High on the vaulting as though levitating,
for five centuries I have gazed down
at a blur of straining adam's apples,
gaping nostrils and goggle-eyes focusing
on the frescoes for long enough to take in
my soft colour tones, my wings' pale
transparency, my fingers on the strings.

Against the hair-line cracks in the sky,
faded through the ages, only traces remain
of my halo's gilding. But no disruption
of my features, thanks to my master
having properly prepared his pigments
before drawing my curls and straight nose-line,
the powdery red and green of my costume.

Not just the fee (though that filled his belly),
or religious conviction. I'll tell you a secret.
Invisible from ground level is a small smudge
on my cheek. His last brush-stroke complete
and before they dismantled the scaffolding
my master leaned up and kissed me gently.
After all those years, that still sustains me.

IX

The Breakfast Room

The Duck Shooters

We count the minutes to departure, the train crammed
to capacity. Across the platform another, its windows
blank, is tenanted if at all by ghosts. 'All passengers

please move to the train opposite.' The original
seating plan preserved, but in our new element,
soon in skuffed plushness we are heading south

within sight of the coast, conversation muted
until instinctively we lean forward in anticipation
of the silvery half-circle of the Basin, a glistening

haven for wildfowl and birdwatcher, habitat
of grebe and oystercatcher, redshank and plover.
As we slow to a crawl, mute-swans deferentially

upend. Then when least expected there appears
a pair of duck shooters, discordant in their relation
to land and water. Barrels raised, it is as though

they are looking not into the train but through
its windows and out the other side, the refracted
brightness of sea and sky rendering us illusory.

Conundrum

You'd think there would be a neat equation for how
when travelling by train the view from the window
and in the mirror opposite make clear we are hurtling
away from the past, and into our future, at precisely

the same speed. Simple you say, stating the obvious.
But it doesn't explain how images, as they recede,
may enlarge in the memory; tunnels ahead shorten
or lengthen in accordance with changes of mood.

Even more how an intrusive cell or invisible speck
between sets of nerves can have an impact more
catastrophic than a rock fissure in a mountain ravine;
the tremor of an eyelid, cataclysmic as any fault-line.

Just How It Was

Will there come a time when looking back
we'll say to one another, that's just how it was –
'how it was' being exactly how, today, it is;
the sun at precisely that angle over the trees
in whose shadow a blackbird is being tracked
by a cat, while from next-door's garden a ball
goes bouncing into the lane; the ice-cubes
in our drinks, meanwhile, remaining icy? Even
then we realised that on entering what was still
the future the ice would melt, the sun duly set,
rendering your ribboned straw hat redundant.
And these essential questions: whether the ball
bouncing into the road would reach infinity,
or the blackbird end up being caught by the cat.

The Camellia House

Clear as though it were yesterday he sees
the tangled entrance to the camellia house,
its dank water-butt, cracked window-panes,
discarded tools rusting; inside, the glory
of the blooms – each waxen flower-head
symmetrical, the colour of blood.
He takes her one each day in season. Her
workmates, oblivious of the walled garden,
the estate where he rents a cottage, thought
he must be really keen. Only she knew
their origin, that no way could he afford them.

Early on St Valentine's day he found
a scene of desolation, beds trampled,
stems crushed and broken, bulldozers
moving in, blocks of flats going up
where the derelict big house had been.
He imagined droves of young lovers
without two pennies to rub together
kneeling to their partners, purloined
flower in hand – rather than concede
that behind the camellia house, might be
a mound of mulched flower-heads rotting.

Dougalston
(i.m. JMSA)

In those long autumn evenings we played carpet bowls
on the huge lawn, growing so engrossed that our game
would extend beyond even the lingering Scottish twilight
thanks to the insertion of a candle in a pound jam-jar
as a substitute for the jack; the contents of a half bottle
taking the edge off the chill; our efforts increasing until
the hurled china bowls would bound off one another
to be lost in surrounding shrubbery; the ultimate delight
when a direct hit, to triumphant whoops, smashed
the jar to smithereens, extinguishing its flickering light.

Rain, Rain, Rain
(for Tom Pow)

Your card tells how you and your son,
holidaying in the Hebrides, experienced
'rain, rain, rain, then glory' – triggering
in my memory forked lightning, lochans
thrashed by demonic claymores, a carbon
fibre trout-rod jettisoned on the machair;

or caught in a freak mid-summer storm,
hailstones drumming on corrugated tin,
drenched cattle looming like water-kelpies,
our fleeing helter-skelter for the shelter
of the black house where we were staying,
its thatch soggy under flapping tarpaulin.

Swamped by these thoughts my mind,
seeking the balm of sunshine, is lured
to that baking afternoon at Benbecula
airstrip and the tannoy announcement,
'Would embarking passengers please
remain in the departure area meantime'

while a group of men in black suits
and dark glasses crossed the tarmac
as the incoming plane taxied closer,
then in what might have been a scene
from a Fellini film, stood watching
a coffin being lowered from the hold

and placed in a limousine: all under
an incinerating sun. From somewhere
nearby the stifled sobbing of women
renders us intruders on age-old ritual.
Recoiling from the image and its clarity,
I long for submergence in 'rain, rain, rain'.

Homecoming Scotland

There we were sipping Pimms with a group of Americans
here for The Gathering, when in came such a man-mountain
I swear the room darkened. Eyes like beacons, he told us

he and his tattooed mate were from Austin, Texas. Between
them, they've traced their ancestry to Wallace and the Bruce:
a shoo-in for tossing the caber, or as tug-o'-war anchorman.

Later our host said, 'I saw you chatting to our gay couple.
Bob – the one with the kilt like a marquee – we call him
'the Buachaille'. Their ambition's to start up a guest-house

somewhere in the Highlands.' I eagerly await the sight
of those massive hands serving the full Scottish breakfast,
or cradling a clutch of speckled eggs, in soft dawn light.

Gondola

We had seen black keels in the nearby
boatyard but this is crocus yellow, its
seating a bare cross-strut – the only one
we've come across, are perhaps likely to.

Soon, adapted to the span and height
of some gondolier, its braided cushions
and gleaming lacquer-work will grace
the Grand Canal. Guided by supple

muscle, long may it stay the course, ride
the *acqua alta*, above all prove watertight:
our wish for ourselves, too, as we steer
into the current, bearing life's freight.

Early Call

There are days when the fear of death
is as ubiquitous as light...
TED KOOSER

Hearing the phone I am loath to answer,
preferring to be closeted from the world's
ills. But when an upstairs neighbour says
there's a woodpecker on our seed-feeder
we speed to the window in time to catch
its black and white stripes and crimson
nape-patch before it flies off: a few more
rings, we'd have missed it. Now all seems
back to normal...unless the small birds'
shrillness signals the sparrow-hawk's return.

The Breakfast Room

Bonnard frequently placed the most important objects on the periphery of a picture.

PIERRE SCHNEIDER

1

That poster has been on my wall for years.
The other night a woman appeared in it,
a nondescript figure, more a housekeeper
than the wife whom the bohemian in him
painted in her bathtub, over and over down
the decades. Holding a cup, the other arm
slack, she merges with the curtains' muted
tones. A balustrade, shady garden beyond.

Waif-like, half her body outwith the frame,
she seems almost spectral, as if dissolving
or part of a transformation scene. I'd gladly
join her: brioches and baguettes to share,
tea in the pot, a chair easily drawn up. But
unlikely, given her forlorn stare. Not once
has there been a prelude to an invitation,
or the least indication she has noticed me.

2

Whether the artist's wife or his châtelaine
why in heaven's name would I invite you in?
You scarcely endear yourself by dismissing me
as some drab. That, or a moody phantom.
While I make no claim to beauty, a little
sensitivity wouldn't come amiss. It can be
hard enough dispelling the notions of those
who ogle my husband's nude studies of me.

As to not noticing you, quite the reverse.
I'm far too aware of your presence, my room
lit at all hours while you pursue your obsession;
loud music putting an end, albeit temporarily,
to my tranquility. But between marginality
and impermanence lies a fine distinction.
Whichever of us you believe to be the fiction,
I'll look out long after you've stopped looking in.

3

You find my Marthe unobtrusive? For a spell
she was so self-effacing, whenever I wanted
to paint her she would hide behind the curtain.
In one portrait not dissimilar to this she virtually
disappears. Here, simultaneously concealed
and revealed, she blends in perfectly. Small
compensation for what she has undergone,
illness held in abeyance by immersion in water:

hence my depictions of her as Venus emerging,
the light casting a spell on her skin as it was
when I first met her. A vision of young love
preserved, my palette imbues her with the blue-
violet of memory. No need to choose between
smelling the scent and plucking the flower –
painting her has been like bottling a rare spirit.
Now, if you'll excuse me, I have her bath to run.

Delivery

Customarily I rise early and spend
a couple of hours in my study before
washing and shaving. One morning
last week, the postman catching me
in night attire, I explained I'd been

up for ages, rhyming away. Today,
exercising, I was perspiring freely
when the bell rang: he eyed me
impassively, then went on his way
murmuring, 'Heavy work, this poetry!'

Sleepless Knight

He shifts uneasily. The turret window, slightly
ajar, casts a slat of light across the four-poster

to reveal his wife sleeping by his side, her silk
nightdress puckered at the neck, and so still she

seems scarcely to breathe. With a sigh he places
a chill hand on hers; overhead her family motto,

'*amor vincit omnia*'. As the weather-vane goes
kiu-kiu like a little owl, or vice-versa, she moans

in her sleep, decorously as is expected of the lady
of the manor. Other small sounds, scratch of quill

on parchment, liquid gently poured, scarcely
register as with a gasp he laboriously raises

his crossed legs to allow just enough room
for the insertion of a small lion to rest his feet on.

Awakenings

When he rose and turned the light on
there it was draped over the bedstead,
a chimera complete with lion's head,
goat's body and dragon's tail. Fearing
the worst he wondered how he could
shield himself from its fiery breath,
only for it to fade away, not the rag-end
of a dream so much as bearing witness
that for their own protection, the least
belligerent of creatures can look fiercest.

Meanwhile she lay petrified, staring
at a tiny fluttering on the ceiling,
not a death's head but some minute
nondescript variety she could obliterate
with a smear of her thumb but at whose
presence her gorge rose, as she recalled
her mother taking the little woollen top
from its tissue paper and how as she put
it on and was buttoning it up it began
to move, full of the eggs hatching.

Double-take

One of the things about old age is that your memory begins
to go a bit, and also, that your memory begins to go a bit.
CLEMENT FREUD

It is snowing, of that I am certain. Falling between us
as we stand on the platform, making of her features
a strange pointillisme, if that is the correct expression.

She stands surrounded by bags, a leather portmanteau
and what looks like an old-fashioned hatbox, while
the carriage doors are being slammed. In the old days

a porter would have offered assistance, but these times
are gone. The difficulty, though, is that I've no idea
whether I'm here to collect her, or see her on to the train.

Amidst a hissing of steam, she is instantly enveloped
in impenetrable whiteness. A chance to run for it?
But too late. A whistle blows, and the train has gone.

When the smoke clears, I am alone on the platform.
A poster on the wall of the waiting-room opposite
shows a woman standing amidst her luggage, an onyx

cigarette-holder in one languid hand, her opal eyes
fixed on me in a way I do not begin to understand.
In the background, a train is pulling either in or out,

Back home, and finding the table for some reason
set for two, napkins pressed, a bottle of Sancerre
chilling, it is clear I must have been expecting someone.

But all I can think of is to start thumbing yet again
through my old timetables, to track down which train
she could've been on, and whether arriving or leaving.

The Loving-cup

The coffee-mug I keep for such occasions
as writing this poem flaunts a floral pattern
bounded by bands of umber, a sticker on its base

saying 'souvenir Firenze'. It replaces one from an earthy
Fife pottery whose handle sheered without warning,
other predecessors having variously had their day –

one pressed on us by a waiter in a Burano *trattoria*
in whose voice we'd traced Edinburgh cadences,
now a repository for pencils and quill-feathers;

another from the University of Western Illinois
stamped 'recycle' and 'contents may be hot';
and a ceramic goblet, smashed and restored, fit

for display only: reminders of places visited, decades
dispersed or, gathering dust, marking our passage
through the stages of marriage. Rarest of all

the twin-lugged loving-cup with our initials
intertwined, unbreakable because imagined,
brimful of memories that can never spill.

Early Morning

You know the feeling – when rising early
and about to start work you become aware

of a distraction: not the customary
juddering of an adjoining water system,

shift of masonry behind the panelling,
nursery rhymes through the wall;

more a slightly asthmatic snoring,
but mellifluous and in perfect rhythm.

Has an inner partition been taken down,
some somnambulist moved in?

I throw open the shutters, let light in.
There they are on the garden wall,

the male cooing like a benign steam engine,
the females all a-do. A rap on the pane

and they've gone, clumsily as befits the elderly.
Next morning they're back, amorous as ever.

This time I leave them in peace. Worse things
to have outside your window than so decorous a love-in.

Arcadia

Having down the years grown accustomed
to the brown-and-white plates and sauceboats
on your kitchen shelves, the other day I took in
for the first time their Arcadian scenes. The *pièce*

de résistance, an ashet eighteen inches across,
shows reclining if not Dame Flora then a near
relation, in a coach drawn by prancing hounds;
behind a Doric arch, a girl with a bow and arrow.

Long unnoticed, they are blissfully oblivious
of the aromas and bubbling pans, never mind
the dinner-talk, the concertos from the radio
on the marble table-top below. But look closely,

on tiptoe if need be, you'll see the chariot
she's in has only two wheels, so that she defies
gravity the way only a beautiful woman can –
and as our lives hope to, through love's sway.

Coolly she ignores the leap to the quarry-tiles
below. Less secure I ponder that given
a sudden tremor, our Arcadia could topple
and shatter to shards on the kitchen floor.

Soloist

Seeing above Glen Lyon a forester
sawing in a shaft of sunlight so far

downwind the sound is drowned
by perpetual lark-song, I am drawn

to that sweltering auditorium decades ago
and Rostropovitch playing Dvorak's cello

concerto; folk melody rising, the soloist
silhouetted in a nimbus of gold-dust.

Beaux Arts Trio
(farewell concert, 30 August 2008)

The head of the man in front blots out the violinist
until easing to my right I can see the bow caress
the strings, the pianist's fingers dance across
the keyboard. Now and then I close my eyes

to take in the harmonies. Each time I reopen them
the page-turner leans decorously over, an avatar
offering guidance. After the interval the man's
groomed outline, tilting slightly, induces in me

unexpected benevolence; while his female
companion sways scarcely perceptibly
to the serenity of the *Archduke*, as Beethoven's
jubilation emerges from darkness. The Trio

then run riot in Shostakovich's *Devil's Scherzo*,
wrist movements faster than the eye can follow;
afterwards no mere standing ovation but a storm
of applause, animated hands moving mountains of air.

The Life Ahead

There's no suggestion we don't know who we are
who have, after all, spent our entire married lives
together. But should that day come when either
of us fails to recognise the other, what would I
salvage as a memento of who we once were?

Sunlit slivers of holidays like those in Provence,
lavender and thyme ladling the air, your
legs dandling from a wooden bridge while I tried
to catch swallowtails with a straw hat; allied
to visiting ancient churches and châteaux, tours

of this museum or that; our clinging together
in an icy wind, on the boat back from Torcello;
your elucidating the emotion emanating from
some Renaissance painting; more mundanely,
walking home from the Usher Hall, through

Edinburgh's New Town; threading these, hours
of reading or contemplation, the unregarded
epiphanies of everyday, visits from family
and friends. Our own lives till now charmed
but more and more aware of others on razor-wire,

given the eventuality I should pray above all
that no harm befall you – but to whom, given
there's no God I believe in? Chary of total denial,
I'd cling to the coward's middle way, though
with no more faith than in the mantra *I love you*.

Homecoming

Trying desperately to think what to buy
that will do you justice – not some tawdry
trinket from the market or expensive item
for which I know you won't thank me – I find
my heart speaks for me: why not a dewdrop

at the point of dissolving; this red wine's
bouquet; a note plucked by that guitarist
on the bridge; or from a minaret in the old town,
the moon's reflection? Impossible of course.
Instead, I stuff my suitcase with fresh herbs,

a replica of an antique cup from the Museum
of Macedonia and, knowing your sweet tooth,
a box of Turkish delight. Only to regain my wits
when it's too late. How perfect, an apple picked
in that garden I visited, crisp and succulent,

with symmetrical on its twig, two glossy leaves.
Even that, I discover, would have been redundant,
given the ample boxful friends have handed in.
Nothing for it but resign myself (no great imposition)
to a cosy kitchen filled with sounds of munching.

Sounds of Music

Sitting in our kitchen as I sometimes do,
ruminating, while you have food to prepare
I become conscious of a sporadic humming,
a series of *pom-pom-poms* which I assume
are coming from the CD you're listening to.

Next morning, during the Haydn trio
in the Queen's Hall, there it is again –
this time more an acoustic reflection,
although mercifully the level so low
it might pass as a sympathetic resonance.

But have the musicians caught on? Every
so often they break off, bows poised as if
for confirmation, then resume their *pizzicato*.
Countering my relief there lingers a fear
that were I to mention it, you'd say I do it too.

What if it grew rife among senior concert-goers?
Imagine at this evening's *La Clemenza di Tito*
a communal humming, swelling to *fortissimo*,
drowning orchestra and chorus till Mackerras
turns on the podium, conducts the audience en masse.

Sir Robert de Septvans

Before our marriage and while working in London
my wife, having seen in *Monumental Brasses of Britain*

an illustration of Sir Robert de Septvans, determined
he would be her knightly companion. On an excursion

to Chartham near Canterbury, bearing black heel-ball,
paper and masking tape, she encountered a benignity

beyond expectation: hands held together in prayer,
ring-curls symmetrical, his armorial bearings three

winnowing fans; slender legs decorously crossed,
feet resting on a lion couchant, mane and tail aflame.

The rubbing when completed she had framed and hung
in our first flat, his demeanour unchanging whether

in my small study or the expanse of the front room
with its television screen and sporadic overnighters.

But a tear, scarcely perceptible at first, ate slowly
into his surcoat, severing his sword-arm. Hesitant

to dump him on a skip, we rolled him in a cylinder
marked SIR, unsure what the future may hold for him

or ourselves, for whom he spanned half a lifetime;
and whose *in memoriam* he may unwittingly become.

Carpe Diem

From my study window
      I see you
below in the garden, a hand
      here pruning
or leaning across to snip
      a wayward shoot,

a daub of powder-blue in a
      profusion of green;
then next moment, you are
      no longer there –
only to reappear, this time
      perfectly framed

in dappling sunlight, with
      an armful of ivy
you've trimmed, topped by
      hyacinth blooms,
fragrant survivors of last
      night's frost.

And my heart misses a beat
      at love for you,
knowing a time will come
      when you are
no longer there, nor I here
      to watch you

on a day of such simplicity.
      Meantime let us
make sure we clasp each
      shared moment
in cupped hands, like water
      we dare not spill.

X

New Poems

On the Viaduct

Our train approaches the estuary, the tide
out. A quivering skin of weed and water,
frilled at the edges, distorts the distant hills.

Those familiar figures with their fowling pieces,
have they gone to ground? Do they reload
behind the dunes, or did they encroach only

in the mind? And this sense of having
been here before: was it as children
or with lost loves long reduced to ghostly

presences? No chance to find out: picking
up speed we tilt with the line's camber,
in the smeared windows the sheen of sky

and open sea, our lives held momentarily
in abeyance while the arches of the viaduct,
and the land beyond, pull remorselessly away.

Revenants

All it needs is for that cloudless
patch of blue to re-emerge, the fluffy
white vapour-trails be reconstituted,
fragile cherry-blossom reaffix itself,
bruised fruit be whole on the bough,
the kamikaze fledglings return safely
to the nest and that pair of stupefied
bumble-bees to loll on their backs
and have their furry bellies stroked.

That's all. And our younger selves
to be revivified as in those early
photos, you in your striped skirt,
me in that silly hat, the rocks taken
from one of our favourite colourists,
the tide perpetually half-in, half-out –
and of course, those specks scarcely
visible on the skyline to be not mildew
but a school of dolphins making whoopee.

Knowing the Code
(for David and Mim)

Not until the third occurrence
did they relate the 'Bright Star'
announcement over the tannoy

to members of the crew heading
for this or that cabin, among them
a matronly figure with gold-rimmed

glasses and sad eyes. When at
breakfast next morning they enquire
after the sallow gentleman who had

202

joined them for meals previously,
the steward murmurs, 'I'm afraid
he passed away, yesterday.'

Knowing the code, and with so
many among them aged or infirm,
by the umpteenth fiord they are

familiar with the practice. Now
reclining in deck-chairs, the ice
in their glasses tinkling, their nightly

ritual is to gaze upward, wondering
will they detect any increase in
the tenancy of the starry heavens.

Juggler

This time last year I stood in the Meadows
watching a boy in a saffron tracksuit

juggling three tennis-balls, then after
a stroll round Arthur's Seat, found him

tireless on the same spot. Early
this afternoon he reappeared,

looping five oranges high in the air.
As pointless to ask him why, as for him

to enquire why I'm writing this poem,
each in endless search of perfection,

the marriage of inspiration and design.
But which is rehearsal, which the real thing?

And what chance one day of Chinese
lanterns floating, diaphanous, over the trees?

An Absence of Crocuses

(for Wendy)

Sacks of crocus bulbs due for delivery
to the Park held promise of a profusion
of purples and yellows, only for a sudden

snowfall to preclude their planting.
That afternoon we learn of the death
of a friend we've known for years.

As the first swallow is a sign of spring
so on her arrival would our Festival
really begin, laughter at outrageous

puns rocking the kitchen, gifts
of Cumberland sausage sizzling,
crosswords found mysteriously filled in.

Intrepid traveller and fell-walker
while still able, and ardent pursuer
of Ring cycles, next year's absence

of crocuses will be a simple symbol
of her loss for those who loved her.
The snow meantime steadily

makes a lacework of our cherry tree;
a reminder how, in Japanese culture,
white, not black, is mourning's colour.

Field Marks

(*JMSA*)

The bulk of what I retain I learnt through him,
from that trek to Flanders Moss in the hope
of seeing a grey shrike on a blackened tree-fork,
to a pair of hen harriers whose upward glide

made him beam with pleasure. His first
ringing-trap dismantled (it attracted vermin),
he designed and built one that bears his name
on the Isle of May; while in the cottage we shared,

coffee-mugs and cigarette-butts cleared,
and like as not whisky glasses from chess
the night before, he'd set up his carousel
of colour-slides to display the field marks

of various species – pointing out such features
as eye-stripes and wing-bars, nesting habits
and flight-patterns – or draw lightning sketches,
his profile more and more that of a raptor.

One tip I recall: on my return from Blaven
wondering could I be sure I had seen a golden
eagle, he took me benignly to task: 'You know
it's an eagle, when you don't need to ask.'

Nocturne

Unlikely anyone else views you as I do
from a window overlooking our garden

while unravelling this book of haiku,
and I'm pretty sure no one imagines

you their secret geisha about to serve
sushi, sushami and other delicacies

with ivory chopsticks, the evening
sky a parasol of shot silk. Certainly

not our neighbours, any more than
I'd presume on their privacy,

though catching them squinting at
the crescent moon, I hope they take in

the comeliness of our cherry tree. Nor
are they naïve enough to share my vision

of you in a kimono or believe that blackbird
is chirping Bashō, which as darkness

thickens has begun tchinking in distinctly
Scottish mode, and is no longer to be seen.

A Hair in the Gate

Whenever they shot the perfect scene
he would hear the cry, 'There's a hair
in the gate, stand by to take it again'
and like as not end up distraught, the light
fading, the cast's concentration gone. Then
his thoughts would turn to the wintry day
when crouched behind a dry-stane dyke
clutching his first box Brownie, he'd seen
that snowy-white creature, ears pricked,
and in the split second before it lolloped off,
clicked and caught it, a perfect hare in the gate.

In the Garden

I was young just minutes ago.
MAURICE SENDAK

Seated in the garden he hears supper being prepared,
metal trays sliding from the oven, plates and cutlery laid.
The voices though muted he hears too, as if alive, their
timbre and tone recalling loved ones long since gone.

Though they cannot repossess what was once their own,
at any time he could join them, the past slipping seamlessly
into the future, himself as intermediary. This makes him
concentrate all the more on the present, the scent of lilac

and lily-of-the-valley merging into a single sweetness,
in the distance the cries of children playing, somewhere
a heavy sash window lowered and as the air chills,
an unfamiliar muskiness enveloping him, like fine ash.

Wellcome

My plans exist in my mind like a jigsaw puzzle...
and gradually I shall be able to piece it together.

SIR HENRY WELLCOME, 1853-1936

As though a neolithic arrowhead he unearthed
at the age of four had entered his bloodstream,
its sliver of flint sparking an obsession, the items
he acquired over the years ranged from Darwin's
whalebone walking-stick, Napoleon's toothbrush
and a pair of Florence Nightingale's moccasins
to shrunken heads and tons of ancient armour.

But despite all his squirrelling, the museum
to house them remained illusory. Picture him,
his explorer's garb and trappings laid aside,
increasingly hemmed in, until overwhelmed
by the mouldering mountain, moth-eaten,
worm-ridden, filling his Willesden warehouse
to overflowing, he ended up part haunted,

part devoured by more than enough to fill five
Louvres but not some insatiable chasm within.
Garlanded and afforded the scholastic kudos
he craved, a vast fortune securely amassed,
did he at the last find respite from cupidity
or in a lonely hall of mirrors, cower from those
behemoths hemming him in, their foetid breath?

Irish Giant

Imprisoned in a glass case, my flesh
boiled away, to satisfy the curiosity
of every Tom, Dick or Harry is not how
I dreamt of spending Eternity; but despite
my constant pleas to be buried at sea
John Hunter – the 'pioneering surgeon'
they still call the unscrupulous
bugger – snatched me for his collection.
Almost two centuries I've been housed
in this Museum, subject to the vagaries
of the human psyche: some stand in awe
of my great height, others gawk as at a freak,
forgetting they are but lesser versions of me,
or turn away, I like to think out of decency.
Every so often a group of youngsters
will snigger and nudge one another;
but seldom do I detect a vestige of pity.
Medical research served, and my DNA
saved for posterity, why can't they
release me and commit me to the deep –
not confined in a lead casket but allowed
to weather like an old hulk, my ribs
its curved and sprung timbers, scaly
luminosities nestling in my crevices,
under the billows, at last to find peace?

Off the Leash

Three dogs come bounding down Porty prom,
twisting and cavorting as they leap the barrier
and go splashing along the dowdy tide-line,
their balletic exertions suspended in air. One
especially, a black and white collie, shows such
superabundance of spirit I am rooted to the spot
as it comes loping and pirouetting towards me,
radiating catherine-wheels of spray. Only as they

go tumbling and somersaulting past do I take in
that the collie, whose explosiveness and defiance
of gravity so caught my eye, has one foreleg
missing, which if anything appears to enhance
its exuberance as it heads, twisting and loping
(not to forget, of course, cavorting and bounding)
back up the prom the way it came, the least trace
of deformity banished by its spirit and grace.

Tide

On that sinuous passage from infancy
and youth's buoyancy through middle
life to advanced years, the one certainty
is a gathering of momentum consistent
with time's flow – something scarcely
uppermost in my mind as the trout
I'm playing draws me downstream
till rocked by the tidal undertow I fight
to retain my balance: hard to know
where the river ends and the sea begins.

Off Iona

At the time of the Reformation the monastery
beside the burial-place of kings was destroyed,
all but a few of three hundred and sixty
stone crosses thrown into the sea, to form
something between an untenanted *cimetière
marin* and a vault for giant chessmen; the runic
inscriptions and intricate scroll-work on those
which survived, MacLean's and St Martin's
the finest, a reminder of what had been lost.

Leaning over the prow I imagine them resisting
the undertow, tangled fronds manacling them
in place, communities of mussels and limpets
bedded on them; while squid-like creatures
clutch at our keel, attempting to drag us down,
entrap us with them, till the day of Resurrection.

Estuary

Waking in the small hours the night
before you go into hospital, you press
the palm of my hand to your cheek
so that my wrist, following the line
of your neck, detects its pulse-beat,
making me aware as though we were
on the sandy foreshore of some vast
estuary of the tide's tug, and precious
grains slipping through my fingers.

Fisherman

Having over the years warred with the elements
and pitted himself against fractious currents
never mind the fish themselves, cast downwind
or into a choppy gale with equal dexterity,
his preference always for dry, quick to cover
a circling fin glimpsed out of the corner
of his eye, patience part of his philosophy
and stoically phlegmatic any time one
got away, it was to no ordinary monster
of the deep that he finally succumbed,
but one whom not even with his trusty rod
and skilled boat-craft he could reel in, yet
whom it goes without saying he resisted
with no murmur of complaint, privacy
and dignity preserved in a display
of such bravery, hard not to imagine
on his coffin his colourful hoard of flies
arrayed row on row, like medal ribbons.

Resolve

All I know is, there must come
times more wondrous which will
set white horses dancing, in our
nostrils the fragrance of far islands.

Sea Crossing

It was one of those rare days when Skye's
coastline could seem almost Mediterranean,
the sea's ribbons of turquoise and ultramarine
no painterly fiction; one of those days you know

instinctively could be once in a lifetime. As the four
of us made the short crossing to Canna, where
we would stride ankle-deep in wild flowers and throw
ourselves gasping on the cliff-top to look down

on a pair of sea-eagles wheeling, even then –
long before in a stupor of heat and exhaustion
we returned to Drinan and I was handed a gin
and It with a kick that would've knocked

a highland bull for six – there was a sense
that today, in many ways indistinguishable
from any other, nonetheless had a uniqueness
stemming not least from perceived interweavings

on the journey of our lives. So it came about
that everything seemed shared but contained;
the harmony of setting, the venison, the moon
within arm's reach, a lighthouse blinking

across Loch Slapin, inducing a well-being
not tied to the moment; as though the soul,
beyond the transience governing ourselves
and our loved ones, really were eternal.

Italian Suite

In the Basilica

Having spent what seems hours marvelling
at the apse's mosaics-meadow, the bejewelled
golden cross with its haloed creatures lapped

in soft light from the alabaster windows, not
to mention the fluted pillars whose evangelical
figures look as though they'd spent centuries

poised for just this moment, and of course
the glow of the intrados, sensing that even
you have surely reached saturation point,

I turn towards the beckoning exit only for you
to grasp my arm and say, in undiminished
wonder, 'The floor's really worth looking at, too.'

Train journey

On the return journey from Ravenna,
the interior is warmed by the setting sun,
long shadows aslant the vineyards.

Dozing off, I bask in the abundant
afterglow of those saintly figures,
sheep grazing in radiant pastures,

only to be aroused by the persistence
of a ticket-collector stooping over me,
whispering urgently, 'Signore, signore',

oblivious of how brusquely he disrupts
my sojourn among the Angels, aware only
of an old man's all too mortal slumber.

Urbino

Stepping from the bus we gazed at the walls
and turrets, looking for the sign, 'Ascensore',
then having taken the lift found we faced

a stiff walk to almost the highest point;
upon which I set off jauntily, leaving you
to follow. On subsequent occasions I'd

eagerly go ahead, as if blazing a trail – only
to learn, on our return, of the breathlessness
that had begun increasingly to slow you down.

Whatever the future may hold I realise,
it not being possible to retrace our steps,
essential from now on to travel at the one pace.

In the Palazzo

An indelible image of our stay
is of you leaning forward to study
Piero's enigmatic masterpiece,

its rapt groupings of figures
bathed in crystalline light,
suspended in time and space.

Alone in the room, concentration
unbroken, in that stillness before
the crowds intrude, your presence

adds in a wider frame such intimacy
and dimension as lastingly convey
all that it means to you, and you to me.

Room of Angels

Against an azure background in the Room
of Angels is a frieze of dancing putti, a procession
of chubby cherubs or cloned cupids whose wings

and willies, like their musical instruments,
are delicately gilded, the vivacity of their features
dismissive of the centuries. On our flight home

the cloud-banks' limitless expanse of gold-tinted
puff-balls, or meringues and cream, brings them
to mind; so that before the engines roar and our

descent to terrestrial gloom, they are restored
to their element and true domain; their pipings
and flutings one with the music of the spheres.

Horse chestnuts

What to do, on our return, with these three
burnished chestnuts taken from the leaves
round Raphael's statue in an Urbino piazza:

add them to the contents of a small bowl
(pine-cones from Stravinsky's tomb, others
origin unknown) or keep them apart till I've

written about them? Rolling them on my palm
will I see in them, just as I treasure
sky-blue tesserae as fragments of heaven,

the flanks of a rippling bay, only on opening
my fingers to find them nestling like shrunken
relics from an ancient pawnbroker's sign?

The Rooms of the Sweet Oranges

(Palazzo Ducale, Urbino)

With scented citrus in loggias once
intended for guests we were instantly
at ease in their bright airiness, survivors
of the decline and plunder of centuries.

Back home reading the guide I could swear
to an aroma of oranges, and struck by such
powers of suggestion head for the kitchen
to top up my coffee only to laugh out loud

on finding you adroitly doing the peeling
and slicing for a fruit compote, its fragrance
evoking those ornate rooms so intensely
it must surely be more than happenstance:

a reminder, say, that those blissful
days of late summer giving way
to autumnal chill, on our first and maybe
last visit, should not be treated simply

as part of an indiscriminate past
unspooling with ever greater rapidity
but, added to memory's trove, flavour
the remainder of the life we share.

Upholstery

The sofa in our sitting-room, long the worse
for wear, is newly back from an upholsterer
by royal appointment who announces
that to preserve the cachet of age, "old money"
insists on less padding; whereas rather
than boast a pedigree of bottoms, ours
curves in the centre like dough rising.

A couple of days later we read how
the couch in Freud's consulting room
so sags under the weight of over a century
of recollected terrors, phobias and dreams
an appeal has been launched for its repair:
of greater interest surely, to retain the imprint
of the Wolf Man and those hundreds of others?

Fox

Since dawn my binoculars have been trained
on a vixen burrowing frenziedly in a cage
at the foot of next door's garden. When
the pest control man appears, he cloaks
himself in a brown blanket, to mask the kill.

Now the cubs, too, have gone: vermin
after all, the passageway still stinking.
Yet I retain a sense of connivance, unable
to dispel the memory of that hooded form,
cross between a ghoul and a crazed Capuchin.

Hydrangeas

In broad daylight a black girl in a white
dress crosses the street to caress one
of the tubbed hydrangeas burgeoning
on our front steps. On tenterhooks
behind net curtains, until she gracefully
recedes I fear she may snip a flower-head,
strip the plant bare even, provide all
in her troupe with a sumptuous corsage.

Such exoticism scarcely outdoes the claim
of one neighbour, then in her nineties,
that a Ghanaian woman on moving in
transformed our front room into a haven
for damaged birds, central a lime in leaf,
where crows' broken wings could mend
before their release on the lawn, pairs
of mallard squittering on the floorboards.

Such malodorous squalor long since gone,
all we'd faced on a preliminary recce
were lobster-creels stacked in the porch,
the seller about to embark on a career
as a fisherman up north, but facetiously
seen as a severe case of rising damp;
and in our term, no more than vagrant foxes
and squirrels, a sparrow-hawk on the clothes-line.

No way of guessing what may be ingrained
of ourselves and our perceived eccentricities,
from a vulgar Victorian longcase to the stone
lion with blue glass eyes sited in the garden;
or whether, some ultimate owner vacating
the premises, the hydrangeas still all the rage,
a wan household god, no one left to preside
over, will pluck a bloom to adorn his cortège.

Interloper

He reappears dishevelled as ever,
still believing his purloined quill
decorates my inkwell. Awkwardly

flopping he struts the window-sill,
blotting out the light as I work away,
doing my best to ignore him, not easy

given the constant *krawing* at my ear,
until giving up on me, with a venomous
gleam in his eye he winks meaningfully

at his minders on the fruit trees, then
drawing attention to his missing pinion
launches himself lopsidedly into the air,

leaving me to continue in more orderly
fashion, while he and his brigand band
get on with hauling the sun across the sky.

Three Poems for Ellis

I *Celebrants*

The hitherto pent-up song-thrush
in our shrubbery relays the news
that mother and son are both well.

May you, assured of loving nurturing,
grasp in these tiny yet perfect
hands whatever the future may bring

and the world, no matter in what crazed
manner it may spin, do you no harm
but provide solace and protection.

Meantime in the family Bible the section
recording the passage of the generations
awaits your name's neat inscription.

II *Visitors*

Others are praised for their rich plumage
and fancy call-notes, but this bullfinch
settling in next door's garden will do fine
for me, his trademark white rump, red hue
and whirring-in-air a show-piece of nature –
while the arrival of another, more complex
and marvellous, is announced by a ring
at our front door: who knows but some day,
one may be dazzled by the other. Meanwhile
let us love him for what he is, regardless
of whether he ends up noted for his song
and acrobatics or like the homely sparrow,
keeping our peckers up, sociably chirpy.

III *Stone lion*

Among fragments of debris dispersed
on the muddy verge of the walk-way –
vandalised or stolen from a nearby garden,
no way of knowing – lay the head and torso
of a yellow stone lion with blue glass eyes.

A shame to let it lie, I returned next day
with an old rucksack and after a wobbly
cycle-run, found it a shady spot under
our cherry tree, an *al fresco* addition
to our accumulated *lares et penates*;

guardian of the precinct, enabling me
at any hour to look down at those eyes,
imperialist, like fixed stars. No greater
contrast than with yours at just four
weeks, dark pools as yet unfathomed,

while the world waits for you to find
focus and subject ourselves to scrutiny.
So great the expectation, as you mature.
On you meantime, as the years slip by,
be all the blessings the gods can muster.